I0062958

MARKETING
STRATEGIES
FOR
EVERYONE

...

EVERYTHING YOU NEED TO KNOW
WITHOUT HAVING TO KNOW EVERYTHING

SCOTT HARKEY AND AMY COLBOURN

SCOTT HARKEY AND
AMY COLBOURN

Vol. 3

MARKETING
STRATEGIES
FOR
EVERYONE

EVERYTHING YOU NEED TO KNOW
WITHOUT HAVING TO KNOW EVERYTHING

KM PRESS

Phoenix, Arizona

If you purchase this book without a cover, you should be aware that this book may have been stolen property and reported as "unsold and destroyed" to the publisher. In such case neither the author nor the publisher has received any payment for this "stripped book."

This publication is designed to provide competent and reliable information regarding the subject matter covered. However, it is sold with the understanding that the author and publisher are not engaged in rendering legal, financial, or other professional advice. Laws and practices often vary from state to state and country to country, and if legal or other expert assistance is required, the services of a professional should be sought. The author and publisher specifically disclaim any liability that is incurred from the use or application of the contents of this book.

Copyright © 2024 by Scott Harkey and Amy Colbourn. All rights reserved. Except as permitted under the U.S. Copyright Act of 1976, no part of this publication may be reproduced, distributed, or transmitted in any form or by any means or stored in a database or retrieval system without the prior written permission of the publisher.

Published by KM Press

KM Press
15170 N. Hayden Road
Scottsdale, AZ 85260
480-998-5400
Learn more at: www.kenmcelroy.com

979-8-9895781-4-6 (Print)
979-8-9895781-5-3 (E-Readers)

Printed in the United States of America

OTHER TITLES IN THE KM PRESS FAMILY OF BOOKS

KEN MCELROY

ABCs of Real Estate Investing
The Secrets of Finding Hidden Profits Most Investors Miss

ABCs of Buying Rental Property
How You Can Achieve Financial Freedom in Five Years

ABCs of Property Management
What You Need to Know to Maximize Your Money Now

Advanced Guide to Real Estate Investing
How to Identify the Hottest Markets and Secure the Best Deals

The Sleeping Giant
The Awakening of the Self-Employed Entrepreneur

Return to Orchard Canyon
A Business Novel

BLAIR SINGER

Sales Dogs
You Don't Have to Be an Attack Dog to Explode Your Income

Team Code of Honor
The Secrets of Champions in Business and in Life

Summit Leadership
Taking Your Team to the Top

Little Voice Mastery
How to Win the War Between Your Ears in 30 Seconds or Less and Have an Extraordinary Life

JOHN MACGREGOR

The Top Ten Reasons the Rich Go Broke
Powerful Stories That Will Transform Your Financial Life . . . Forever

RICH FETTKE

The Wise Investor
A Modern Parable About Creating Financial Freedom and Living Your Best Life

MIKE MALONEY

Guide to Investing in Gold & Silver
Protect Your Financial Future

CHAD KERBY AND TK STRATTON

Speak and Get What You Want
Communicate Like the World's Most Successful Leaders

STRATEGIES SERIES

Legal Strategies for Everyone
The Complete Guide to Covering Your Assets, Maximizing Wealth, and Protecting Your Family

Tax Strategies for Everyone
How to Slash Your Taxes and Build Wealth

Sales Strategies for Everyone
Essential Selling Tips From the Sales Coach You Wish You Had

Marketing Strategies for Everyone
Everything You Need to Know Without Having to Know Everything

NEW AND COMING SOON FROM KM PRESS

Real Estate Strategies for Everyone
Ten Great Ways to Get Started in Real Estate Investing

KM PRESS

DEDICATION

To the advertising greats who came before us
and to our colleagues of yesterday, today, and tomorrow.

TABLE OF CONTENTS

INTRODUCTION TO MARKETING   xi

CHAPTER 1: The Business   1

CHAPTER 2: Target Audience   33

CHAPTER 3: Research and Data Analytics   51

CHAPTER 4: Branding   69

CHAPTER 5: The Marketing Plan   97

CHAPTER 6: Digital Marketing   113

CHAPTER 7: Advertising and Promotions   129

CHAPTER 8: Creative   147

CHAPTER 9: Sponsorships and Event Marketing   163

CHAPTER 10: All the Other Stuff   173

CHAPTER 11: Marketing Round-up   189

GLOSSARY   193

SOURCES   197

INDEX   199

ABOUT THE AUTHORS   205

INTRODUCTION TO MARKETING

In this book, we've considered and addressed real questions and issues from business owners like you.

Let's begin with marketing. Simply stated, marketing is the activity of promoting and selling products or services and involves many activities, such as conducting market research, creating sales strategies, networking, and advertising. Marketing is essentially an ecosystem of activities, all aimed at getting your products or services in front of customers in meaningful ways. This requires making and then executing an effective plan. One of the most important parts of this process involves branding.

While this all sounds simple enough, the real question is how companies like yours can make sense of it all and apply it to your business. Let us show you how.

We'll walk you through a step-by-step process in straightforward language, none of which must be done in the order it's presented. Apply aspects most useful to you, in the order that works for you. If you're new to this process, start from the beginning.

The Marketing Process

Marketing is the process of promoting, selling, and distributing products or services to customers. This involves understanding customer needs and preferences and then developing and delivering products or services that meet those needs.

Marketing requires a pricing strategy, as well as making the products and services available through sales and delivery channels to reach consumers.

It is also essential to create awareness about the products or services through advertising and other promotional activities, communicating a reason for the consumer to buy them.

Marketing encompasses a wide range of activities, including market research, product development, pricing, advertising, sales, and customer service. The goal of marketing is to attract and retain customers, generate sales, and contribute, ultimately, to the growth and profitability of a business.

In today's world, marketing has expanded to include online and digital marketing strategies, such as social media marketing, search engine optimization (SEO), email marketing, and content marketing. These strategies leverage the power of the internet and technology to reach a wider audience and engage with customers in new and innovative ways. Regardless of all the new technologies, it's essential to understand marketing basics.

Making Sense of Marketing

The most daunting aspect of marketing involves orchestrating a variety of activities aimed at promoting and selling. The most successful marketing strategies often involve a combination of these activities, tailored to the specific needs of the consumer and the goals of the business. The trick to it is understanding which ones make the most sense.

It can seem a little overwhelming to be able to grasp all of the tools available to businesses in the digital age. This book is meant to guide you to better understand some of the core fundamentals:

- Various activities that make up a successful marketing plan
- Process of developing a plan that suits your business needs
- Individual aspects of a marketing plan
- How to maximize elements of a plan so that they can work together

You can choose to adopt some or many of these components based on the individual needs of your business. Use what will work for you.

Why We Wrote This Book

Big-brand advertising can be intimidating. These companies, typically well-funded, can afford to partner with sophisticated agencies teeming with specialists. Not everyone has the benefit of multimillion-dollar budgets or global agency partnerships; therefore, this book is tailored to the needs of small-business owners.

Speaking of budgets, there are a few points we should get out of the way now:

- Marketing is an investment, not an expense.
- The amount to invest in your marketing should represent a percentage of your revenue. We will go into that in more detail later and provide some rule-of-thumb percentages based on your industry.
- When it comes to marketing, you should always operate with a budget in mind. That enables you to make decisions about the best way to go about allocating your budget. Otherwise, you are simply wasting time.

We know the tried-and-true benefits of solid marketing efforts. We also understand the pitfalls of trying to do too much with too little.

Our aim is to help businesses like yours find scalable efforts that drive results.

There doesn't have to be a sophisticated or scientific approach to everything when it comes to marketing. In fact, we can help you become a little more of what we call "scrappy," when you need to be. "Scrappy" describes someone who is determined, resourceful, and willing to work hard to persevere, despite limited resources or support. It means being resourceful in finding ways to uncover information and identify solutions, which come in handy when you don't have unlimited resources.

You don't have to fend for yourself when it comes to marketing. Rather than settling for someone who doesn't have the skill set, experience, or your best interest in mind, take some time to learn the basics.

Understanding marketing is essential for today's business owners. It works when done right. However, it can also burn cash fast, and we don't want that to happen to you. When marketing is done incorrectly, it's blamed for not working—and that gives marketing a bad reputation. We'll teach you how to effectively use your marketing budget.

Keeping It Simple

To help explain a complex topic or to highlight additional insight into a subject, we've included tip boxes throughout the book with easy-to-understand information and advice offered at a glance. These callouts will help guide the discussion and are easily referenced later on when you want to revisit a subject. Throughout the book, you will find these five types of tip boxes:

AHA!
Quick helpful insights

PRO TIP

Pieces of advice from the experts—many times, the things we've learned the hard way through firsthand experience

WARNING

Common mistakes and pitfalls to avoid

E-FYI

Helpful online resources

CLARITY

A piece of clarity that influences the outcome

We've also included **worksheets**, which include supplemental information that can be used as a guide and as the framework for formulating your own plans.

1

THE BUSINESS

This is a book about marketing, but what comes before marketing is as important as marketing itself. We understand that there is excitement and eagerness about taking a brand to market. And there is almost a gravitational attraction to offering as many things to as many people as possible. Resist the temptation to be all things to all people. There is a saying in advertising: "When you try to be everything to everyone, you become nothing to everyone." This means that by failing to differentiate, your business blends into the background. The best brands know what they are, what they offer that is better than anyone else, and who they appeal to. Know this about your business, too. In this chapter we'll show you how.

Chick-fil-A is loved for its chicken and is an example of a company with a clear purpose and set of values. Though it also offers a breakfast menu, it still sticks to its core strength: chicken sandwiches.

Many of the company's values are influenced by the Christian religious beliefs of its late founder, S. Truett Cathy (1921–2014), a devout Southern Baptist. He was known for his servant leadership, great generosity, and reflecting a commitment to letting his employees set aside one day to rest and worship if they chose—all Chick-fil-A restaurants are closed for business on Sundays. This is true today and remains core to the brand's values. We'll talk more about Chick-fil-A and its advertising later.

Brands with a strong sense of self are better prepared to make decisions and stick to them. Brands without a strong sense of self tend to stray from being focused—on audience, product, position— and end up undifferentiated, unsure, and confusing to customers.

A quick note about "brands": We will use "brand" throughout the book as a general reference to a company, product, or service.

Getting Started

Starting is often the hardest part of any type of planning. Knowing how or where to start can seem daunting and overwhelming. We recommend starting somewhere. Get your thoughts, ideas, and information "on paper" and worry about editing, paring down, and organizing the information later.

To help you with planning, we have provided templates for organizing information and to serve as starting points.

Desmond Tutu once said, "There's only one way to eat an elephant: a bite at a time." As this saying states, you don't have to eat an elephant whole; rather, start by breaking your plan down into parts.

Your Checklist for Building a Business Foundation

A strong foundation provides stability and support, whether in building structures, developing skills, or creating a business. It enhances resilience, facilitates growth, and forms a reliable base to work from. Without a strong foundation, marketing is a fruitless effort.

This chapter is about the foundational elements needed to define and set the plan for your business. It includes these key elements:

- **Forming a business model:** A business model outlines how the company creates, delivers, and captures value.

- **Writing a business purpose:** A business purpose provides clarity about why the business was founded.

- **Understanding mission, vision, and values:**

    o The mission is the organization's current purpose.

    o The Vision outlines the organization's future aspirations.

    o Values represent the principles that guide the organization's behavior.

- **Writing a business plan:** A business plan defines goals and outlines how you plan to achieve them.

- **Writing a business proposal:** A business proposal is used to solicit funding in a way that is meaningful to investors and a bank.

....

VALUE IS ALWAYS FROM A CONSUMER POINT OF VIEW

How to Define Value for Your Business

Value is always derived from the consumer point of view (POV). Consumer value is the perceived benefits and satisfaction that consumers derive from a product or service in relation to its cost. These perceptions are subjective. Consumer value is derived from the exchange between what people will gain and what they are willing to give up for what they will gain. This value exchange is what influences purchasing decisions.

....

AHA!

A purchase decision is based on a simple idea: the exchange derived from what people are willing to pay for what they will gain.

CLARITY

A clear definition of your business—and the business you're in—serves as a guiding principle, steering your organization toward success by making informed decisions, fostering innovation, and building strong, long-lasting relationships.

Gaining Clarity on Your Business

What is the purpose of your business?

Every business has a purpose. Defining it enables you to gain clarity on your business and provide guidance in decision-making. The elements covered in this chapter are the essential foundational building blocks. Without clearly defining your business upstream, you can't expect your marketing to be effective downstream.

Gaining clarity around purpose means defining what you do and how you do it better than anyone else.

A Business Model

A business model is a framework that outlines how a business creates, delivers, and captures value. The elements that make up your business model will be captured in the business plan, so there is no need to confuse things and treat them as separate concepts. If you have an established written business model, that's great; we'll plan to use that information to frame your business plan.

What Business Are You (Really) In?

When forming a business, it is typically required to provide a legal definition of your business. These can be vague and broad so that you're not tied to a specific product or service offering. While the legal definition is one thing, what we're talking about here has to do with marketing. And because marketing is all about connecting with the consumer, you will need to understand the consumer and understand what value your business delivers to the consumer. Define what business you're *really* in; this is a shift you must make after the legalities are set up and you're ready to start talking about marketing. What does your business mean to the people who consume what you're selling?

If you sell soft drinks, you are technically in the beverage business. But when it comes to the consumer's perspective, you may consider your business a different type of business delivering a different value. Businesses can fall into the trap of defining themselves by the products they sell, and usually those products are commodities that can be easily duplicated. For example, if you sell soft drinks and you are Coca-Cola, you are in the refreshment business. Here are some other examples of how brands move beyond the commodity to define the business that they're *really* in.

Brand	Product	The Business They're In	The Business They're *Really* In
Coca-Cola	Soft drinks	Beverages	Refreshment
Dollar Shave Club	Personal grooming	Razors	Community
Dove	Personal care	Beauty	Confidence
USA Today	News	Publishing	Content

Business Purpose

You know the reason you formed your business. As it relates to your business plan, it's important to boil down the purpose of your business into a single sentence or two to gain clarity: the real reason you're in business.

WORKSHEET

BUSINESS PURPOSE

....

Here is a quick worksheet to help you organize your business pur-pose using a heating, ventilation, and air conditioning company as an example:

- ☐ **What does your business do?**
  Sells, repairs, and installs residential HVAC systems

- ☐ **Who does your business do it for?**
  Homeowners

- ☐ **How does your business help those people?**
  By making their homes comfortable

- ☐ **What business are you in?**
  Comfort

As an example, Crayola's business purpose is to unleash artistry in children.

It's equally important to understand what a purpose is not. In the Crayola example, Crayola's purpose is not to make money, and it's not to sell crayons. It's much more than that for the consumer. Crayola simply creates the instruments to deliver on its business promise.

Much like the Crayola example, a good brand purpose is inspir-ing. A great brand purpose drives future innovation for the company, and in Crayola's case, both consumers and employees understand the brand has a clear goal of driving creativity in children.

It's sometimes easier to see brand purpose in large national or global brands. For regional or small businesses, your reason for being is also important. It's your why, your North Star. It's why you do what you do and the reason people want to do business with you.

E-FYI

Check out Simon Sinek's TED Talk, "How Great Leaders Inspire Action." It can be found on YouTube.[1] Sinek is also the author of the classic book, Start with Why: How Great Leaders Inspire Everyone to Take Action.

Mission and Vision

You need a clear mission and well-articulated vision.

Mission Statement

The purpose of the mission statement is to provide a short summary of the business purpose and focus. This should be simple enough to stand on its own. A mission statement is a concise declaration outlining an organization's purpose, values, and goals, often highlighting its core beliefs and guiding principles. It serves as the road map for the organization's direction and decision-making.

For inspiration, let's start by looking at some examples of companies that possess a strong sense of self—and a clear mission statement.

- **Amazon:** *"To be the Earth's most customer-centric company."*

- **American Express***: "Our mission is helping others accomplish theirs."*

- **Google:** *"Our company mission is to organize the world's information and make it universally accessible and useful."*

- **Starbucks:** *"To inspire and nurture the human spirit—one person, one cup, and one neighborhood at a time."*

- **Uber:** *"We ignite opportunity by setting the world in motion."*

---

1   https://www.ted.com/talks/simon_sinek_how_great_leaders_inspire_action?language=en.

Vision Statement

Think of the vision statement as a complement to the mission statement and a sight line into the future. It's made up of the hopes and aspirations of an organization. A vision statement articulates an organization's long-term aspirations and goals, providing a compelling description of what the organization aims to achieve in the future. It typically conveys the desired impact or outcome, inspiring and guiding the organization toward its goals. It outlines the goals and outcomes for your business and how it will get there.

Vision is important internally and externally. It is aspirational (about the future) and inspirational (how to get there). It's a rally cry and a manifesto.

To help you find inspiration in forming your own vision, here are some examples of vision statements from well-known brands:

- **ASPCA:** *The vision of the ASPCA is that the United States is a humane community in which all animals are treated with kindness and respect.*

- **Charles Schwab:** *At Charles Schwab, our vision is to be the most trusted leader in investment services.*

- **Ford:** *To become the world's most trusted company.*

- **IKEA:** *To create a better everyday life for many people.*

- **Microsoft:** *To create local opportunity, growth, and impact in every community and country around the world.*

A vision statement is evergreen. So is the mission statement. As your business changes, so do these items. However, it's the combination of business mission, vision, and values that will influence how you make decisions and define the culture you want to create. Let's talk about values.

....

MISSION AND VISION

Here's an easy reference showing examples of brands with their mission and vision statements side by side. It is worth noting that these statements can be subject to change; companies may update them over time to reflect changes in their strategic focus. Italics have been added to emphasize the key points in each vision statement.

Brand	Mission	Vision
Amazon	To offer its customers the lowest possible prices.	To be *Earth's most customer-centric* company; to build a place where people can come to find and discover anything they might want to buy online.
Apple	Apple designs the best personal computers in the world and leads the digital music revolution, defining the future of mobile media and computing devices.	To make a contribution to the world by making tools for the mind that *advance humankind.*
Coca-Cola	To refresh the world through mind, body, and spirit.	To inspire *moments of optimism and happiness* through our brands and our actions.
Disney	To entertain, inform, and inspire people around the globe through the power of unparalleled storytelling, reflecting the iconic brands, creative minds, and innovative technologies that make ours the world's premier entertainment company.	To *make people happy.*

Brand	Mission	Vision
Facebook	To connect people with friends and family, to discover what's going on in the world, and to share and express what matters to them.	To give people the power to build community and *bring the world closer together.*

Business Values

Business values are the fundamental principles and beliefs that guide an organization's behavior, decisions, and interactions. They reflect the company's ethical stance and priorities and the standards it upholds. Values often shape the company culture and contribute to its identity, influencing how employees and stakeholders engage with each other and the broader community. It is really important for your company to understand its values and for your team to embrace them. The values adopted by your team members will ultimately be reflected in how they feel about the company, treat each other, and interact with your customers.

Here are some examples of how different companies handle a different set of values.

- **Google:** Google's "ten things" is a great example of how values can reflect the company internally and externally. Google wrote the "ten things we know to be true" list when the business was just a few years old. Like other elements of a business plan, from time to time, Google revisits the list to see if it is still accurate. Google's list:

    1. Focus on the user and all else will follow.
    2. It's best to do one thing really, really well.
    3. Fast is better than slow.

4. Democracy on the web works.

5. You don't need to be at your desk to need an answer.

6. You can make money without doing evil.

7. There's always more information out there.

8. The need for information crosses all borders.

9. You can be serious without a suit.

10. Great just isn't good enough.

- **JPMorgan Chase:** As one of the oldest banks in the nation, this company is all business. JPMorgan Chase is not a company known for a warm and cuddly, fun-loving culture, nor should it be. That wouldn't be true to its core belief system. Its values are simple and straightforward, conveying how its values focus on honesty, integrity, and ethics.

- **Whole Foods:** Whole Foods breaks its core values into six overarching credos that guide how the company does business no matter what. Whole Foods's values are:

    1. We sell the highest quality of natural and organic foods.

    2. We satisfy and delight our customers.

    3. We promote team-member growth and happiness.

    4. We practice win-win partnerships with our suppliers.

    5. We create profits and prosperity.

    6. We care about our community and the environment.

The approach you take should be authentic to you and your business. Your values will guide how you make decisions and determine the kind of culture you want to create. Customers and employees will know what to expect and what is expected of them, ensuring alignment and avoiding confusion.

WORKSHEET

MISSION, VISION, AND VALUES

··

This table demonstrates a way to organize your thoughts in terms of creating your business mission, vision, and values. A simple way to think about creating and organizing this information is: what, why, and how?

MISSION
What we do:
Write a short summary statement of the business's purpose and focus.
VISION
Inspirational reason for why we do it:
Write a statement that articulates an organization's long-term aspirations and goals.
VALUES
The manner in which we choose to go about it and how we do it:
Write down the fundamental principles and beliefs that guide an organization's behavior, decisions, and interactions.

The Business Plan

A good business foundation is essential before anything else follows. One of the most important elements of a business is developing the business plan. This plan serves as an in-depth look at a company; it helps you measure and guide your business goals and also outlines a company's goals, as well as the strategies for achieving those goals.

A business plan serves as a road map for the success of your business. Creating this plan is important for these reasons:

- **Clarifies business concept and objectives:**
  - Helps clearly define your business idea, mission, vision, values, and objectives
  - Forces you to think through the details and to define goals

- **Guides in decision-making:**
  - Provides a framework for making informed business decisions
  - Helps you anticipate potential challenges and create plans to overcome them

- **Attracts investors and lenders:**
  - A requirement for seeking funding from investors or loans from financial institutions
  - Shows that you have a solid strategy and clear understanding of the market and feasibility for success

- **Demonstrates viability:**
  - Requires that you conduct market research and analyze the competition
  - Helps you to demonstrate the viability of your business idea and identify potential risks

- **Defines target audience and marketing strategy:**
  - Requires you to define your target audience and create a marketing strategy
  - Critical to understanding how to reach your customers and differentiate your business from the competition

- **Financial planning:**
  - Includes financial projections, helps you estimate start-up costs, revenue, and expenses
  - Essential for managing cash flow and ensuring the financial stability of your business

- **Sets milestones and benchmarks:**
  - Includes specific, measurable goals and milestones
  - Helps you track progress and adjust strategies as needed

- **Facilitates communication:**
  - Provides a tool that can be shared with stakeholders, employees, and partners
  - Ensures that everyone involved is on the same page

- **Encourages accountability:**
  - Creates a documented set of goals and strategies to hold you accountable
  - Aligns everyone on the same page and helps hold your team accountable to the plan

- **Adapts to changing circumstances:**
  - Provides a structured framework but offers flexibility to adapt to changes in the market, industry, or other internal factors
  - Is evergreen; regularly revisiting and updating your plan enables you to stay current, agile, and responsive

Setting Goals

Setting goals provides direction, motivation, and a clear path for growth. You may have heard of the term *SMART goals*. SMART is an acronym that represents a framework for setting effective goals. SMART stands for:

Specific

Measurable

Achievable

Relevant

Time-bound

We're fans of this framework, as it provides a structured and memorable way to approach goal-setting. Following this guide helps you create clear and actionable objectives for individual or business goals. Otherwise, it's difficult to accomplish what you need in order to reach the desired result. Let's break down each component.

- **Specific:** Clearly define the goal so that it's easy to understand.

  Example: Instead of setting a general goal like "increase sales," set a specific goal such as "increase online sales by 15 percent within the next quarter."

  This is equally as effective in setting individual goals. Instead of setting a goal like, "lose weight," a specific goal would be "lose five pounds in the next two weeks." The specificity makes it more achievable. It sets a target that you can visualize.

- **Measurable:** Establish criteria for measuring progress, and determine when the goal has been achieved.

  Example: Instead of a vague goal like "improve customer satisfaction," a measurable goal would be "achieve a customer satisfaction rating of 90 percent or higher on the next customer survey."

This also provides guardrails for your project that you can adjust as you see fit during the process. Knowing that goals may be adjusted makes it likelier that you will achieve that goal. Back to the weight-loss example, let's say you only lose four pounds in two weeks, instead of achieving your goal to lose five pounds in two weeks. This scenario shouldn't discourage you. Instead, it's an opportunity to reset your measurement for the next two weeks to align with what you think you're able to achieve.

- **Achievable:** Ensure the goal is realistic and attainable, given the resources and other factors.

  Example: Instead of setting an unrealistic goal like "doubling your customer base in one month," an achievable goal might be "increase the customer base by 20 percent over the next six months."

  Think of it this way: It's much better to hit an achievable goal than to set an unrealistic one.

- **Relevant:** Confirm that the goal aligns with broader objectives and is relevant to the business.

  Example: Instead of setting a goal that is unrelated to the overall business strategy, such as a lighting company striving to "become the leading supplier of agricultural equipment," a relevant goal would be "launch a new product line to meet the growing demand for sustainable products in the market." This feels more relevant to what your business can achieve and is in tune with your customers and the market landscape, which are all components of relevance.

- **Time-bound:** Create a time frame for achieving the goal, providing a sense of urgency and deadline for completion.

  Example: Instead of leaving the timeline open-ended, a time-bound goal would be "reduce production costs by 10 percent within the next fiscal year." Having a date in place creates a sense of urgency; having the end goal in your sight line makes achieving the goal more realistic.

Adopting the framework for setting SMART goals can have a positive impact on all areas of your life. This approach increases the likelihood of success and helps the tracking process. On the other hand, unrealistic and undefined goals without a time frame can feel out of reach and unattainable, as well as overwhelming and discouraging. After all, it's nearly impossible to hit a target you can't visualize!

What Is a Business Model?

A business plan is different from a business model.

A business model is more about how a company operates. It describes how a company creates, delivers, and captures value. This leans into revenue streams, cost structure, key resources, and channels.

Whereas a business model is specific to the methods and procedures of a company, a business plan is broad and inclusive of elements of the business model. A business plan is a critical tool for strategic planning, management, and achieving long-term success in a business venture.

The business plan is strategic, and the business model is fundamental.

What Is a Business Proposal?

A business plan is also different from a business proposal.

A business proposal is essentially a pitch to potential investors to help support a business venture. We sometimes refer to this as an "investor pitch presentation" or simply "investor pitch." It consists of all elements needed to convince an investor to take a bet on your business being successful so that he or she will want to make an investment in your business. It shows that you have anticipated the risks and assumptions and have carefully thought through an approach.

How to Create the Business Plan and Proposal

In this chapter, we will discuss both developing a business plan and a business proposal.

The advantages of starting with a business plan are that many aspects of the business plan can be realized in an investor pitch or marketing plan.

Here's an effective outline for a business plan, with each section explained.

Business Plan Outline

- **Executive Summary:** This is a brief overview of the entire business plan.
    - o Put the Executive Summary first in your business plan, but complete it last. It's your "elevator pitch" about your business.

- **Company Overview:** This is the overview that explains what you are (really) selling and in which category. An overview includes:

  o *Business Description:* An introduction to the product, its purpose (your "why"), and the market it aims to serve.

  o *Vision and Mission:* A clear statement of the mission and the vision.

  o *Management and Organizational Structure:* Information about key team members, their roles, and the organizational structure. This may include an organizational chart, along with biographies for the executive team.

- **Market Research and Analysis:** These elements demonstrate you've done your homework and clearly understand the market and the opportunity for your business to thrive. This part should include:

  o *Market Landscape:* An overview and understanding of the market geography and/or the market category or industry.

  o *Target Audience:* A snapshot of the people your business will appeal to the most. This is the audience that possesses the greatest opportunity to buy what you are selling. This is the decision-maker. An effective way to envision the target audience is to think about the person with the greatest level of influence over the buying decision.

  o *Competitive Analysis:* An overview of the immediate competition, including its competitive advantage, claim, call to action, positioning, tagline, and unique features. A firm grasp on the competition enables you to find the "gap." We call this a "gap analysis." It means finding the gap that no one else in your category has claimed.

....

FIND A GAP IN THE COMPETITIVE LANDSCAPE, AND FILL IT

The most successful brands are able to define a consumer need and fill it. A gap analysis is a fancy way of saying, find out what each of your competitors represents, find what's missing—or the gaps—and find the way in which your brand fills a gap. You can get scrappy with this just by doing a routine review of competitor websites to see what they're saying about themselves. What we mean by "scrappy" is being resourceful with something that doesn't necessarily have a scientific method. If competition, including is claiming that they have the best customer service, maybe you can claim that your brand is the most trusted one. If all of your competitors are claiming that they offer the best value, maybe you can claim that your product is of the best quality.

Walmart, for example, may not offer the most options; however, Walmart's claim is to offer "Everyday Low Prices" and to provide value to customers through cost-effective products and services. Walmart owns low prices in the category; when a consumer thinks of low prices, they think of Walmart.

....

- **Products and Services:** This pertains to the features and benefits your product or service offers to consumers. Let's break this down for you:

  o Features are the specific characteristics or attributes of a product or service. They describe what the product or service is or has. For a smartphone, some examples of features might be the screen size, processing speed, camera specifications, and storage capacity.

  o Benefits are the positive outcomes or advantages that customers gain from using the features of a product or service. They explain how the features fulfill the needs or desires of customers. Using the smartphone example, benefits might include high-quality photos, fast performance, and being intuitively easy to use.

- **Marketing and Sales Strategy:** This is a separate project. Later in the book (Chapter 5), we'll address how to write a marketing plan. For now, it's important to understand the key elements of the marketing and sales strategy that should be included in the business plan. They are:

  o *Marketing Plan*
    This is a comprehensive document that outlines a company's overall approach to marketing to reach your goals and includes the strategy (how you will do it) and tactics (with what you will accomplish it). One really great way to look at a marketing plan is that it addresses goals for the long-term (decades) using strategy for the near term (a year), tactics in the short term (quarterly), and effort frequently (daily). A plan serves as a strategic tool to guide a company's marketing efforts and provide a framework for efficient use of resources. This is a critical component of the broader business-planning process. Expect the development of the marketing plan to require an effort of its own. We have dedicated a chapter to understand each element and how to go about the planning process.

  o *Go-to-Market Strategy*
    For new brands, or brands new to market, a go-to-market strategy is another comprehensive plan that outlines how a company will go about bringing its products or services to market. It defines how it will reach its target consumers. We'll cover this more in Chapter 5, as it is a specific type of marketing plan. Much like a marketing plan, it involves a combination of marketing, sales, distribution, and communication strategies designed to introduce something new. Its goal is to maximize market penetration, create awareness, drive revenue, and establish a competitive edge in the market and among consumers.

o *Pricing Strategy*

We've touched on the idea of consumer motivation as a value proposition; this is another way of saying what the customer is willing to pay for a product or service. The value proposition is the value of the benefits to the consumer. What does this have to do with a pricing strategy? It has everything to do with how you price your products or services, and it all depends on what consumers are willing to pay. Establish a pricing strategy that aligns with the perceived value of the product or service in the target market (the place where it is available to consumers). You will want to consider factors such as competitor pricing, customer willingness to pay, and overall market conditions.

o *Sales Approach*

Your sales team and approach to sales are critical to your business model and distribution network. Some businesses have a sales team (like window replacement companies), others have retailers (like lotteries), and others are sold directly to consumers (such as fashion brands), also known as direct-to-consumer. Understand your sales team, treat them like one of the audiences you must communicate with, and provide them with the tools and resources needed to effectively sell your products and services. This may include training, promotions, sales incentives, sales collateral, and customer support materials. There are several common sales and engagement approaches that we will address later in this book. See Chapters 9 and 10 for information about sponsorships, event marketing, and more related topics.

- **Funding request:** If seeking investment, this includes details about the amount of funding required.
  - A business plan will be needed to approach a funding request. Whether from investors, bank lenders, or other sources, this requires careful planning and a well-thought-out proposal. This business plan helps investors better understand your business and revenue expectations. People don't want to invest in things they don't understand—that feels uncomfortable and comes across as risky.
  - Financial statements should be accurate and up to date. They should include revenue projections, income statements, balance sheets, and cash-flow projections. This information helps demonstrate the financial health of your business and is an essential element to complement all the more conceptual branding and visionary aspects of your business.
- **Appendix:** This is a great place to include additional details and ancillary information. We've found that an appendix is a great tool that enables you to be focused with the up-front information in the presentation without sacrificing the details. Other information typically doesn't belong in the body of the proposal. The proposal must be concise. You can place extra content in the appendix. Things to include in the appendix are:
  - *Risk Analysis:* Assessment of potential risks and mitigation strategies
  - *Marketing and Promotion:* Plans for promoting the product or service
  - *Operations Plan:* Day-to-day operations, management, and staffing

Keep the business plan concise, get straight to the point of what your product or service has to offer. People have limited time. It may take a few versions to get to the meat of the information, and that's okay. Writing a business plan is a process. A basic template for a business plan follows.

WORKSHEET

THE BUSINESS PLAN TEMPLATE

···

A business plan is a comprehensive document that outlines the goals, strategies, and operations of a business. It serves as a road map for the business, guiding its growth and development.

EXECUTIVE SUMMARY

Purpose: provides a concise overview of the entire business plan

Components:

- ☐ Business concept and mission statement
- ☐ Summary of products and services
- ☐ Business structure and ownership
- ☐ Key financial highlights

BUSINESS DESCRIPTION

Purpose: offers a detailed explanation of the business, its mission, and its goals

Components:

- ☐ Company name, location, and history
- ☐ Mission statement
- ☐ Vision statement
- ☐ Business goals and objectives

MARKET ANALYSIS

Purpose: examines the industry, market trends, and competition

Components:

- ☐ Industry overview
- ☐ Target-market analysis
- ☐ Consumer demographics and needs
- ☐ Competitor analysis

ORGANIZATION AND MANAGEMENT

Purpose: details the structure and key personnel involved

Components:

- ☐ Business structure (e.g., sole proprietorship, partnership, corporation, LLC)
- ☐ Organizational chart
- ☐ Key management personnel and their roles
- ☐ Board of directors or advisory board

PRODUCT OR SERVICE LINE

Purpose: describes the products or services offered by the business

Components:

- ☐ Detailed description of products or services
- ☐ Unique selling points
- ☐ Intellectual property considerations

SALES AND MARKETING

Purpose: outlines the marketing and sales strategies

Components:

- ☐ Marketing plan
- ☐ Sales strategy
- ☐ Pricing strategy
- ☐ Promotion and advertising plans

FUNDING REQUEST

Purpose: specifies the amount of funding needed and its use

Components:

- ☐ Funding requirements
- ☐ Use of funds
- ☐ Financial projections

FINANCIAL PROJECTIONS

Purpose: provides a forecast of the business's financial performance

Components:

- ☐ Income statements
- ☐ Balance sheets
- ☐ Cash-flow statements
- ☐ Break-even analysis

APPENDIX

Purpose: includes any additional information and supporting documentation

Components:

- ☐ Resumes of key personnel
- ☐ Letters of recommendation
- ☐ Market research data
- ☐ Legal documents (e.g., contracts, permits, trademarks)

STRENGTHS, WEAKNESSES, OPPORTUNITIES, AND THREATS (SWOT) ANALYSIS

Purpose: evaluates the business's strengths, weaknesses, opportunities, and threats

Components:

- ☐ Internal strengths and weaknesses
- ☐ External opportunities and threats

☐ Strategies to capitalize on strength and opportunities while mitigating weaknesses and threats

IMPLEMENTATION PLAN

Purpose: details how the business plans to execute its strategies

Components:

☐ Timelines and milestones

☐ Responsibilities and key personnel

☐ Action plans for marketing, operations, and other key areas

RISK ANALYSIS

Purpose: identifies potential risks that may affect the business

Components:

☐ Identification of key risks

☐ Mitigation strategies

☐ Contingency plans

Business Proposal, AKA the Pitch Deck

A business proposal may also be described as a "pitch" (or "pitch deck"), as it is a presentation to potential investors in search of support for a business venture. It aims to set the vision, frame the potential, and appeal to the audience for funding support.

Put on your sales hat, because it's important that you look at a business proposal in this way: You are selling a concept to investors. This means developing a compelling and realistic view of your business, including all of the background information needed to form a case and demonstrate potential value to investors. You only have seconds to make a good first impression. This means you have to have a strong selling proposition and you must get there quickly.

Airbnb's founders used a pitch deck to raise $600,000 from investors in 2008. The pitch deck outlines Airbnb as a solution for booking rooms with local individuals rather than hotels. It identifies problems with traditional hotels, such as high prices and feeling disconnected from the local culture or places. The solution presented a website where users can rent out spare rooms and spaces to travelers, enabling guests to save money while experiencing a place through local connections. Market validation shows strong interest in temporary housing options, and the business model calls for a commission on each booking transaction. The competitive advantages include ease of use, listing a space once and renting it many times, and incentives for hosts. The pitch deck outlines the opportunity and potential for the business to succeed.

As an example, following are the first three slides from the Airbnb pitch deck.

WELCOME

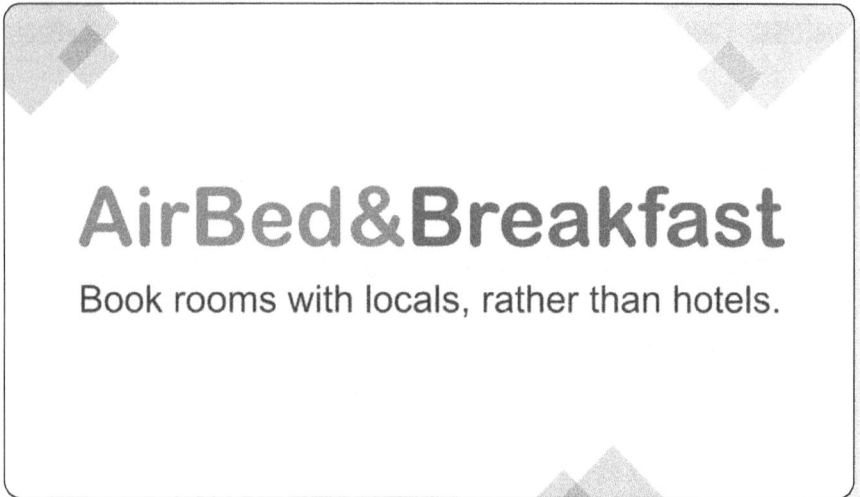

AirBed&Breakfast

Book rooms with locals, rather than hotels.

PROBLEM

Price is an important concern for customers booking travel online.

Hotels leave you disconnected from the city and its culture.

No easy way exists to book a home with a local or become a host.

SOLUTION

A web platform where users can rent out their space to host travelers to:

SAVE MONEY	MAKE MONEY	SHARE CULTURE
when traveling	when hosting	local connection to the city

Once you've completed your business plan, congratulations! That's one of the most difficult things to do. Next comes the business proposal, or "pitch deck," which will simply build on what you've already created, with some added nuances to appeal specifically to investors.

Here's an effective outline for a business proposal with each section explained.

Business Proposal Outline

- **Introduction:** Briefly introduce your company and the purpose of the pitch.

- **Problem Statement:** Explain the problem your product or service solves.

- **Solution:** Describe your solution and how it addresses the problem.

- **Market Opportunity:** Provide data on the market size, growth potential, and target audience.

- **Business Model:** Explain how your company plans to make money.

- **Traction:** Highlight key milestones, customer testimonials, or partnerships to show progress.

- **Competitive Analysis:** Analyze your competition, and explain your unique selling points.

- **Marketing and Sales Strategy:** Describe how you plan to acquire and retain customers.

- **Team:** Introduce your team and its qualifications.

- **Financial Projections:** Present financial forecasts, including revenue, expenses, and funding requirements.

- **Ask:** Clearly state what you're asking from the investors (e.g., funding amount and terms).

- **Use of Funds:** Detail how you intend to use the investment.

- **Appendix:** Include any additional relevant information, such as product demos, case studies, or market research.

Remember to keep the pitch deck concise and engaging, focusing on the most compelling aspects of your business. If you already have one, it's always a good idea to find ways to make it better. We hope this provides some inspiration for improving your pitch.

We've provided a template for a pitch deck below to help get you started in case you don't already have one.

WORKSHEET

THE BUSINESS PROPOSAL TEMPLATE

....

Below is a one-page template for a business proposal showing multiple slides for a visually appealing presentation-deck format.

- ☐ **Slide #1: Welcome.** State what the business is in one sentence.

- ☐ **Slide #2: Problem.** State the consumer problem your product or service solves.

- ☐ **Slide #3: Solution.** Describe how your product or service solves the problem.

- ☐ **Slide #4: Market validation.** Demonstrate the demand for your product or service in the market.

- ☐ **Slide #5: Market size.** Show the potential for sales or revenue to be generated within a specific market over a defined period.

- ☐ **Slide #6: Product.** State what the product or service is.

- ☐ **Slide #7: Business model.** Describe the way the business operates.

- ☐ **Slide #8: Market adoption.** Describe the ways in which customers begin to purchase and use new products or services.

- ☐ **Slide #9: Competition.** List the businesses that offer similar products or services within the same market.

☐ **Slide #10: Competitive advantages.** Display the unique strengths or advantages that your business has that will enable you to outperform the competition.

☐ **Slide #11: Financial ask.** Detail the funding amount and terms.

☐ **Slide #12: Use of funds.** Describe how you will use the funds to invest in the business.

PRO TIP

Build your business proposal in a presentation-deck format. Slides force you to use less copy, which means you will spend more time focusing on developing a clear and concise presentation.

Consider following the 10/20/30 rule for making presentations:

- *Ten slides*
- *Twenty minutes*
- *Thirty points (font size)*

In Summary

✓ *All good marketing efforts begin with a solid understanding of your business.*

✓ *The best way to begin a business plan is by getting your thoughts on paper.*

✓ *Points of clarity about your business can, and will, be applied down the road.*

✓ *Branding and marketing are ultimately about defining value for your product or service and communicating it in order to encourage action.*

2

TARGET AUDIENCE

Target audience is just a fancy way of saying the people who may buy what you're selling.

Whether your business is targeting other businesses (B2B) or consumers (B2C), they all have one thing in common: people. You are selling to people, so you need to understand people. We have dedicated an entire chapter to identifying and understanding the audience.

AHA!
We don't do business with businesses; we do business with people.

All marketing begins with the consumer.

The easiest way to think about why the audience is so important is to think about why products and services exist. They exist to solve problems for people. The problems may be real or imagined, and they may be considered essentials or luxuries, but either way, they all fulfill a perceived need. We will discuss the aspects of understanding the people who form our consumer audiences.

Topics include understanding:

- Why an audience is essential: a marketing must-have is understanding people

- Human behavior and emotions: why people do what they do, their pain points, and their motivations

- Consumers: the people who may buy what you're selling

- Identifying target audiences: exactly whom you should be targeting for sale of your products and services

Why an Audience Is Essential

Just like a performance, it's important to understand the audience. A puppet show is targeted to children, while an opera may be targeted to a more mature audience. Audience relevance makes the performance connect with the people who are watching and the experience more pleasurable. The same goes for selling products and services; your audience consists of the people likeliest to want and use what it is you're selling.

Who the Audience Is Not

You! Whether you want to believe it or not, chances are that you are not the audience. Your friends and family are also not the audience. Don't make the mistake of relying on them to provide feedback and make decisions about your marketing.

WARNING

You must not fool yourself into believing that you are the target consumer. In fact, the customer has a set of pain points and motivators that are likely vastly different from your own. You need to understand them and remove your personal bias from the decision-making and purchasing process.

Understanding the Consumer's Mindset

In branding and marketing, because you are selling to people, you need to understand people. Understanding how people go about making decisions and the factors that influence consumer decision-making are the first steps to sales and marketing.

Consumer decision-making is a complex process influenced by several factors. And once the process is better understood, navigating consumers becomes a lot easier. There are many different models and theories that attempt to explain the process, but boiling it down to the basic principles of decision-making generally involves a few key stages.

- **Recognition of a need or problem:** The process begins with recognition. This could be triggered by internal factors such as hunger or discomfort or external factors like advertising, pop culture influence, or word of mouth.

    o In marketing, we often talk about "framing the problem" to determine the consumer's need so that we can define how the product or service can fill that need. More often than not, commercialization has the ability to create desire based on a perceived problem or need. It has the ability to help people feel valued or fulfill their need to be recognized. Commercialization is all about tugging on the emotional heartstrings that intrinsically make us human.

- **Search for information:** Once a need is identified, consumers seek information to help them make a decision. They may gather information from various sources, including personal experiences, referrals from friends and family, ads, online reviews, and expert opinions.

- **Evaluation of options:** Consumers may take alternatives into consideration when seeking options and to affirm a decision. They assess different options based on various criteria, such as price, quality, brand reputation, features, and personal preferences. This stage involves comparing and contrasting the choices available to them.

- **Purchase decision:** After evaluating alternatives, consumers make a purchase decision. Factors such as price, availability, and convenience can affect this decision. In some cases, external influences such as discounts, promotions, and other incentives can also play a role.

- **Purchase:** The consumer acquires the product or service. The access to acquiring and the ease and convenience of the purchasing process can influence overall satisfaction. It's essential to pay attention to the consumer's purchase experience before, during, and after the actual purchase itself. This is part of the overall experience, which eventually leads to overall satisfaction.

- **Postpurchase evaluation:** After making a purchase, consumers assess their personal satisfaction. If expectations are met or exceeded, it reinforces positive feelings pertaining to the purchase experience, which will likely result in a repeat purchase. If not, it may lead to dissatisfaction and potentially influence future decisions.

There's also a thing called "buyer's remorse". This is the feeling of regret or anxiety that a person may experience after making a purchase, often associated with concerns about the product's value, utility, or their decision to buy it.

Brands can also deliver position associations with purchases after the fact, eitherthrough advertising, brand marketing, or one-on-one communication with customers. The follow-up or experience after the purchase can be very effective in swaying how the consumer feels about the product or service and also influences their decisions to purchase again or make a return visit. People like to feel good about their decisions. Advertising and marketing not only encourages consumers to buy, but they can also have positive effects on the purchase decision.

Once you understand the decision-making process, it's important to understand the contributing factors. This part can be a lot of fun, as it explains how the things around us influence who we are and why we do the things we do.

Let's take a look at the factors that influence people and the decisions they make:

- **Psychological factors:** These include things like motivation, perception, learning, attitudes, and beliefs that all play a role in shaping consumer decisions.

- **Social factors:** Family, friends, culture, habits, traditions, and social class can influence what products or services consumers choose.

- **Personal factors:** Age, lifestyle, occupation, life stage, and personality traits are contributors to decision-making.

- **Situational factors:** The context in which a decision is made, such as the urgency, the need, or the specific occasion, can affect the decision.

- **External factors:** This includes elements of marketing such as advertising, promotions, brand image, brand associations, brand values, and other marketing strategies that can significantly influence consumer decisions.

What's really essential to understand is that the decision-making process is not always linear; rather, it's a complex process with several factors contributing to the outcome. Consumers may skip or repeat certain stages, depending on the complexity of the decision and the individual. Additionally, the rise of online shopping and the availability of information on the internet have altered traditional decision-making patterns, making the process more dynamic and interconnected.

It's also important to note that the decision-making process may occur over the course of several months or even years, especially for large purchases. High-dollar purchases (such as cars, homes, or expensive electronics) tend to require a higher level of consideration.

The process of many stages may be combined into one. With online shopping, for example, awareness, consideration, and conversion may all be combined into one transaction, leading to more impulsive purchase decisions. The process may also consist of greater consideration in advance of purchase, with the availability of more information online through consumer reviews and digital marketing strategies.

WARNING

The target audience is often overlooked, oversimplified, or includes "everyone." ("Everyone" is not a target audience.) Because this is essential to the success of your business, we have dedicated this entire chapter to discussing the target audience.

Now that you have a little bit of a better understanding about the decision-making process and factors that can contribute to it, let's discuss behavior.

Identifying Target Audiences

Your products and services are created to solve problems and fill needs for consumers. The purpose of marketing is to form messages and deliver these messages to people who are likely to buy. In order to do that, you must find out who is likely to buy your products and services, what they want, how you can help them, and how to reach them.

E-FYI

Need help defining your target audience? Now is a great time to use an AI tool, such as ChatGPT, to help define your ideal customer.

Consumers and Their Behavior

Consumer behavior is the study of how people buy, use, and dispose of goods, services, ideas, or experiences to satisfy their needs and wants. It's a multidisciplinary field that draws on insights from psychology, sociology, economics, and marketing. Understanding consumer behavior is essential for businesses and marketers because it helps them identify and anticipate the factors that influence consumers' purchasing decisions. There are several factors that contribute to consumer behavior that are interesting for marketers to understand:

- **Personal factors:** These include individual characteristics such as age, gender, occupation, lifestyle, personality, and values.

- **Psychological factors:** This refers to the internal processes that influence consumer behavior, such as motivation, perception, learning, and memory.

- **Social factors:** Social influencers also play a major role in consumer behavior and include factors like family, friends, social class, culture, and associations that influence consumer choices.

- **Cultural factors:** Culture, subculture, and social class are elements that affect values, beliefs, and behaviors of consumers. Cultural influences can shape preferences and perceptions of products and services.

- **Situational factors:** This refers to the situation in which a purchase is made or the context for making the purchase, such as time constraints, the physical environment, and the purpose of the purchase. All these factors can influence consumer decisions.

Other factors that contribute to consumer buying decisions include the marketing mix and media channels:

- **Marketing mix:** Also known as the 4Ps, this stands for product, price, place, and promotion. The combination of these factors also influences buying decisions. Effective marketing strategies consider the combination of factors and how they meet the needs of consumers as a mix.

- **Social media channels:** We generally categorize social media channels as online and offline channels. The rise of digital technology and online shopping has added another layer to consumer behavior. Consumers are more informed than ever, have more access to customer reviews, and are more influenced by other consumers due to social media channels. Online influences and immediate access to information have significantly changed and shaped how consumers make purchasing decisions.

It's fascinating to study why people do what they do. Studying consumer behavior helps businesses tailor their products, services, and marketing strategies to better meet the needs and expectations of the target audience. More specifically, this understanding enables companies to create effective advertising campaigns, set appropriate pricing strategies, and design products that align with consumer needs and preferences. All this ultimately leads to increased customer satisfaction and repeat purchases.

Emotional Drivers

In 1956, a book written by Victor O. Schwab, *How to Write a Good Advertisement,* described emotions that people want and the emotions that cause people to act. These emotions still ring true today. Despite advances in technology and changes in our lives, there remains a set of basic needs intrinsic to human beings. Whether they make us feel happy, fulfilled, or comfortable, these basic emotional drivers become the foundation for our actions. According to Schwab, these are the drivers that may be of particular interest when it comes to marketing. Below are some of the emotional drivers that cause people to act and that motivate people to take action.

PEOPLE WANT TO GAIN:

- Health
- Self-confidence
- Time
- Improved appearance
- Comfort
- Leisure
- Increased enjoyment

PEOPLE WANT TO SAVE:

- Time
- Discomfort
- Risks
- Money
- Worry
- Embarrassment
- Doubts

PEOPLE WANT TO BE:

- Efficient
- Up to date
- "First" in things
- Proud of their possessions
- Influential over others
- Liked

It's important to understand that people usually buy based on real or perceived needs. Now that you think about it in this way, it's easier to understand how consumers are filling a void for something that is a necessity or not. The desire to fill a need gives people a functional reason why they must buy; however, it really comes down to the fact that purchase decisions are almost always motivated by emotions. In the business of marketing, we must be in touch with the consumer and their emotions. Understand what motivates people to buy, and align your messages with their emotional priorities.

Sixteen Human Emotions

The reason why we're going deep into the emotive side of people is because human emotions play such an influential role in dictating why people do what they do. While there is no agreed-upon list of the intrinsic human emotions, as the classification of emotions can vary across different theories and cultures, this list can help you think about how your product or business delivers emotionally. It's another way of thinking less about pushing product attributes and more of how your brand aligns with consumer values. Here are some commonly recognized basic emotions:

- **Joy:** a feeling of happiness or pleasure
- **Sadness:** a sense of loss or unhappiness
- **Fear:** an emotional response to a perceived threat
- **Anger:** a strong feeling of displeasure or hostility
- **Disgust:** a strong aversion or revulsion
- **Surprise:** a sudden or unexpected emotion
- **Anticipation:** excitement or expectation about future events
- **Trust:** a belief in the reliability or goodness of something or someone

- **Distrust:** a lack of confidence or faith in someone or something
- **Interest:** curiosity or engagement in something
- **Boredom:** lack of interest or stimulation
- **Shame:** a painful feeling of humiliation or distress caused by a consciousness of wrong or foolish behavior
- **Guilt:** a sense of responsibility for wrongdoing
- **Love:** a deep affection and attachment
- **Envy:** coveting someone else's possessions, qualities, or success
- **Pity:** sympathy and sorrow for someone else's misfortune

People are either trying to gain pleasurable emotions or avoid painful ones.

Emotions can be complex and even overlap, and different cultures and psychological theories may have variations in how they categorize and define emotions. Additionally, some researchers argue for a small set of basic emotions, while others propose more extensive lists. What's the purpose of emotions in marketing? It's to understand what motivates people to make the decisions they make. To understand the emotions that dictate behavior. Most purchase decisions are made emotionally and justified rationally.

Seek first to understand and then to be understood. You may recognize this as one of the seven habits of highly effective people introduced by author Stephen R. Covey in his book, *The 7 Habits of Highly Effective People.*

This principle emphasizes the importance of empathetic communication and effective listening in interpersonal relationships. In the context of this habit, Covey encourages individuals to prioritize understanding others before trying to make themselves understood. This involves active listening; putting oneself in the other person's shoes; and seeking to comprehend the other person's perspective, feelings, and motivations. Covey reasons that by truly understanding others, we can build stronger relationships, reduce conflicts, and create a more collaborative and positive environment. By understanding consumer pain points and motivators, we can better align brand value propositions with the priorities of consumers. Simply stated, if we understand what people want, we can position our products and services to fulfill their most burning desires and urgent needs. Fulfilling needs is a lot more effective than pushing product attributes. This notion is simply magical when it comes to marketing.

If you have not yet read Covey's book, please consider moving it to the top of your reading list. His rules for success easily translate into the principles of business and marketing. The bottom line is, the habit is rooted in the idea that effective communication requires not only expressing oneself clearly but also taking the time to comprehend the thoughts and feelings of others. By doing so, individuals—and brands—can foster better relationships and find mutually beneficial solutions to challenges. Understand what they want, and then fill the need. It's that simple.

Demographics

Demographics play a crucial role in marketing by helping businesses understand their target audience, along with the differences and similarities within the population segments they represent.

Demographic profiles provide detailed descriptions of a population based on characteristics. This information is easily found through sources like the U.S. Census Bureau, as well as city, county, and state governments and visitor bureaus.

E-FYI

The United States Census Bureau collects and provides demographic and economic data to understand the changing dynamics of the U.S. population. You can access information online to find out more about the market populations your business serves: https://www. census.gov.

This information analyzes factors like age, gender, income, education, marital status, and location to enable marketers to tailor messaging and delivery strategies to effectively appeal to and reach specific groups of people. This targeted approach enhances the chances of successful marketing campaigns being able to resonate with the people for which they are targeting.

But demographics alone do not determine a target audience in terms of what influences their purchasing decisions. For this reason, we started with the emotive side of purchasing first and addressed demographics second.

Now that we better understand the ingredients, let's build the framework for defining a target audience, step by step.

How to Build a Target Audience for Your Business

Identifying and understanding your target audience is a crucial step in developing effective communication strategies, whether it's for marketing, writing, designing, or any other form of interaction. Most important, please remember that you must define an audience. This means selecting the demographics and profile of the segment of people likeliest to buy your product or service without alienating new audiences. You must not lose sight of your core audience. You must focus on the people likely to purchase your product or service while considering the other persons of influence and/or consumers.

For example, it is a proven fact that adult women in a household are likely to make grocery and health-care decisions. However, in both examples, it is all the members of the household who influence the buying decision and consume the products being purchased.

Below are some fundamental elements to consider when defining your target audience.

Element	Definition	Example
Demographics	Age, gender, location, education, income, and family status	Married, retired, and living more than 60 miles outside of a metropolitan area
Psychographics	Interests, values, lifestyle, and personality traits	Very social and loves to meet for coffee and play tennis, or introverted, keeps his or her social circle small, and plays on a Monday night bowling team
Behaviors	A day in the life, buying behaviors, and media choices	Takes his or her kids to school, commutes to work, and stops at the convenience store on the way home from work
Communication styles	Technology and communication preferences	Email versus text or direct mail versus a phone call, or tone of voice, such as compassionate or direct and to the point
Pain points	Challenges and frustrations	Lack of time and money
Motivators	Goals and aspirations	Health and convenience

By combining these elements, you can create detailed buyer personas or audience profiles that will guide your strategies and help you tailor your messaging to effectively reach and engage your target audience. Keep in mind that your target audience may evolve over time; it's essential to regularly reassess and update your understanding of your audience.

WORSHEET

TARGET AUDIENCE PROFILE

··

These guidelines help you answer questions to define your most important customer: your target audience. When you understand your audience, everything you do is with the customer in mind.

DEMOGRAPHICS

- ☐ **Age:** What is the age range of your audience's members?
- ☐ **Gender:** Are you targeting a specific gender, or is your audience diverse?
- ☐ **Location:** Where is your audience located geographically?
- ☐ **Income:** What is their income level?
- ☐ **Education:** What is their educational background?

PSYCHOGRAPHICS

- ☐ **Interests:** What hobbies and activities are they interested in?
- ☐ **Values:** What principles and beliefs do they hold?
- ☐ **Lifestyle:** What is their day-to-day life like?
- ☐ **Personality:** What traits define their personalities?

BEHAVIORS

- ☐ **Buying behavior:** How do they make purchasing decisions?
- ☐ **Usage patterns:** How often and in what way do they use your product or service?
- ☐ **Brand loyalty:** Are they loyal to particular brands?
- ☐ **Media consumption:** Where do they get their information? Which media channels do they prefer?

COMMUNICATION STYLES

- ☐ **Technology usage:** What devices and technologies do they use?
- ☐ **Online behavior:** How do they interact on the internet and social media?
- ☐ **Communication preferences:** What channels do they prefer for communication? How do they prefer to be communicated with? What tone and style resonate with them?

PAIN POINTS

- ☐ **Challenges:** What problems and challenges do your audience members face?
- ☐ **Pain points:** What are their pain points so you can tailor your messaging accordingly?

MOTIVATORS

- ☐ **Goals:** What are their short-term and long-term goals?
- ☐ **Aspirations:** What do they aspire to achieve?

The Second-Most Important Audience

When it comes to marketing, there's another audience you really need to listen to and understand. That's your internal audience, or your employees. In many businesses, employees serve on the front line, interacting with your customers and your guests. Their ability to deliver on brand and even advocate for your brand is an essential part of your marketing. We'll talk more about research and feedback directed to employees later in the book, but what you need to consider is that your employees are one of your target audiences and deliberate marketing efforts should be targeted at them. These efforts may include things like:

- Sales promotions
- Rewards and incentives
- Awards and recognition
- Brand stewardship
- Personal presentation
- Customer engagement
- News and other communications

Let your employees be the first to know which new products, services, and customer promotions are being introduced so that they are properly trained to represent the business.

You may also need to consider separate campaigns or marketing efforts targeted at recruitment and retention of employees. Having and keeping a good workforce is essential to every business and should be thoughtfully approached. Your approach to your employees can also serve as a competitive advantage in your business. Some businesses are so focused on getting and maintaining customers that they simply lose sight of the people in the organization who make it happen.

This is especially true if you are in a service organization like real estate, lending, roofing, general contracting, and hospitality. Oftentimes, the product that you deliver could be considered a commodity—the same basic product or service available somewhere else. In services, what differentiates the business is the experience or method of delivery. How you deliver the service—right down to each detail—is part of your brand. Your employees should be trained on the nuances of your business so that they can deliver in a consistent manner that is aligned with your values and standards.

Let's take a look at a roofing business. For the most part, roofing products are the same. What distinguishes one company from another usually is price and delivery. And when it comes to the quality of the buying experience, most people are willing to pay more. If a roofing company arrives late and the project takes longer than expected, it creates a disruptive experience for the customer. If the roofer also tramples the bushes and leaves debris in the flower bed, it creates a very poor customer experience. However, the roofing company that arrives on time, delivers ahead of schedule, and leaves the flower beds as good as they were when they arrived, makes the customer happy. In both scenarios, the outcome is the same: a new, warrantied, leak-free roof. Each spends about the same amount of money; yet, one customer is unhappy with the experience, and the other one is satisfied. The satisfied customer is likely to refer their roofing company to friends, neighbors, and family. That roofing company is building a branded reputation and making customers advocates for its business.

The best marketers aren't the ones who know the most about some tool or tactic. The best marketers are the ones who know the most about people.

In Summary

✓ *All good marketing begins with the consumer in mind.*

✓ *Whether it's B2B or B2C, they are people.*

✓ *Understanding human behavior helps position your brand, products, or services.*

✓ *Understanding your audience means knowing exactly who's likeliest to buy.*

3

RESEARCH AND
DATA ANALYTICS

In this chapter, we'll help you better understand types of research and data and what you can do to maximize research. Research can be expensive and complicated. However, it can also be simple and, sometimes, when given a limited budget and time, research can be scrappy.

We'll address some key areas of research that can help you be a better marketer. The more you know, the more you are able to take a leadership position in the market and gain a competitive edge.

> **PRO TIP**
>
> *Whether it's big or small, formal or informal, make research a part of your ongoing marketing process: learn, gain insights, apply, and repeat. Use real information to guide your decisions.*

When to Do Research

Market research should be conducted at various stages of a product's life cycle and also during key points of your marketing strategy development and implementation. Most important, it should be an ongoing process that informs and guides your marketing decisions throughout the entire life cycle of your product or service. Here are some key events for when you may want to consider conducting market research:

- **Before launching your product or service:** Understand your target audience, market trends, competitors, and potential demand for your product or service. This helps in shaping your marketing strategy and messaging.

- **During campaign planning:** Refine your marketing objectives, and identify the most effective channels to reach your audience; understand consumer preferences and behavior.

- **Continuous monitoring:** Measure the effectiveness of your campaign before and after the campaign, identify areas for improvement, and stay updated on any changes in the market or among consumers.

- **Competitor analysis:** Pay attention to your competitors' strategies, positioning, media spending, and performance in order to remain competitive and adapt your own marketing strategies accordingly.

Establishing Baselines

If you haven't done market research before (or your product, service, or business is new to the market), consider conducting market research to establish baselines. This means conducting an initial investigation to understand the foundational aspects before launching something new or while it's in its early stages. Collecting baseline information in the early stages of marketing and media campaigns enables you to track progress from the beginning. Baseline surveys may include market size and growth, target-audience analysis, competitor analysis, market trends, consumer needs, pain points and barriers, distribution channels, and perceptions.

Research can help inform decisions, drive strategies, minimize risk, and maximize effectiveness of marketing efforts. As with marketing, research is an investment and should not be treated as an afterthought.

CLARITY

Learning how to track and analyze customer behavior and data can improve marketing efforts. What gets measured gets done.

Research and data and analytics are closely related concepts; yet, they represent distinct elements in the process of understanding and leveraging information.

Research can help you understand the industry landscape, target market, target audience, and competition. It can help you understand where your business fits into the current market and how your products and services are perceived by consumers. It can also guide product development and improvements to enhance customer satisfaction.

Data and analytics can help you determine what you're doing right and what you may need to change—what's working and what's not.

PRO TIP

- **Research** *is the collection of information and data through various methods.*
- **Data** *serves as the input for analytics, where patterns are identified and insights are extracted.*
- **Analytics** *are a key component of research, helping derive meaningful conclusions from data.*

Let's break down these concepts further so that you can better understand what to use and when it makes sense to use them.

Research is used to gain knowledge, answer questions, or solve problems.

It's a broad process that uses various methodologies—most commonly, qualitative and quantitative methods. Qualitative research is more anecdotal and descriptive, whereas quantitative consists of numerical values that can be measured. Many times, these two methodologies work well together, because they provide information in different ways. Research typically involves formulating hypotheses, collecting and analyzing data, identifying key takeaways, and drawing conclusions.

These common examples of qualitative research versus quantitative research demonstrate the difference.

Qualitative	Quantitative
In-depth interviews to understand consumer experiences with products or services	Surveying 500 participants to measure the relationship between products and their benefits
Observing customer behavior around product usage to understand how consumers engage with products	Analyzing statistics to identify trends
Conducting and analyzing focus-group discussions to uncover customer attitudes toward a brand, a product, or its marketing	Conducting experiments to measure the effectiveness of marketing efforts or product performance
Reviewing textual data from online forums to examine attitudes toward brands	Collecting data on consumer habits to analyze the influence and impact of factors and purchase behavior

AHA!

- *Qualitative information is more about dialogue, and quantitative is more about numbers.*
- *Primary research is the custom research you do yourself—usually more specific to your business—and secondary is existing research that someone else did.*

Primary and Secondary Research

There are typically two types of research: primary and secondary. Primary research involves custom methodologies for data collected firsthand; secondary involves use of existing data. When you use primary research methods, you can focus on the people you want and ask specifically what you want to ask them. Secondary research relies on other existing sources to gather information. You can see there are some instances where you want to control the questions and the audiences and other times when gathering wide-based information from a broader secondary source can help guide your decisions or even guide your primary research.

Primary and secondary data also work well together. For example, you may have industry-specific information available through a trade association that you can overlay with your primary data— say, from a customer survey.

When it comes to research and data, the information alone typically doesn't indicate much without the benefit of interpretation and analysis. The most important part is what you do with the information. It should be applied to create an action plan. Having information is one thing; knowing what to do is another. The purpose of research is to obtain information to help guide decisions. It's the applied knowledge that helps drive the results you want.

Types of primary research include:

- Surveys

- Focus groups

- Interviews

- Experiments

- Observations

- Literature reviews

- Concept testing

Here are some useful sources for secondary research:

- Trade associations
- Convention and visitors bureaus
- U.S. Census
- Academic journals
- Government publications
- Market reports
- Reputable news outlets
- Websites like PubMed, Google Scholar, and government agencies (such as the U.S. Census Bureau and the World Health Organization)
- Platforms such as Statista or Pew Research Center
- Publications like *The World Almanac*

When using secondary sources, it's important to verify the credibility of the sources and check for publication dates to ensure the information is current and relevant. Depending on what you're planning to do with it, it's also important to note sources for reference purposes.

PRO TIP

It's not what you ask; it's what you want to know that matters. And only then it's what you do with the information that matters. Gather information, and then use insights to formulate an action plan.

Data and Analytics

Data refers to raw facts, figures, and information that on its own may lack context or meaning. Data can also be qualitative (descriptive) or quantitative (numeric). Data serve as the foundation for analysis and decision-making. Data are collected, stored, and processed. This information must be processed in order to define takeaways and extract meaningful insights. And much like research, the information alone doesn't mean much without the interpretation applied to define actionable steps.

Examples of data are:

- Customer names

- Purchase amounts

- Survey responses

- Demographic purchase patterns

In marketing, many methods are used to collect data in order to understand customers and buying trends. Methods to collect data may include:

- Customer surveys

- Incentives

- Enter to win (sweepstakes)

- Free giveaway in exchange for contact information

Analytics involves the analysis of data, such as statistical techniques to uncover patterns, trends, and insights. Analytics are used to identify insights, make predictions, and support decision-making. In other words, it helps to understand what has happened, what is happening, and what might happen in the future. Three types of analytics are:

1. **Descriptive:** to understand what has occurred
2. **Predictive:** to understand the likelihood of future outcomes
3. **Prescriptive:** to optimize outcomes based on predictions

Research is the overarching process of investigation, data are the raw information collected during that process, and analytics involve the computational analysis of data to extract insights and support decision-making. All three elements are interconnected and contribute to a holistic understanding of a subject or problem.

For example, let's say we conducted a study about casino patrons and found that they were likelier to visit a local casino on Thursdays, Fridays, and Saturdays. The implication would be that guests are likelier to visit the casino toward the end of the week as a reward. We could use this information to incentivize them to visit on a Monday, Tuesday, or Wednesday by offering a special promotion or giveaway.

Determining What You Want to Know

Now that we have covered the textbook discussion of research and data and analytics, let's discuss ways in which research and data can work for you. If you are going to conduct first-party research, it's essential that you first decide what you want to know. There is a very important distinction between what you want to know and what you want to ask. Determining what you want to know dictates what you want to ask—it doesn't work the other way around. Too often, people launch into listing the questions they want to ask before determining what they want to know.

Once decided, a research professional can work with you to determine the methodology—or the most effective method of getting the information you want in a manner that is statistically accurate, meaning that it's representative of the population.

Professional first-party research can tell you a lot about your brand, products, services, or business. Some examples are:

- Brand perception

- Brand awareness: baseline and brand tracking

- Purchase preference

- Buying motivation

- Consumer buying behavior

- Message testing

The Scrappy Side of Research

Let's move on to the scrappier side of research. Here we'll discuss some ways to get useful information without breaking the bank or taking too much time.

> **E-FYI**
>
> *Create your own online survey using SurveyMonkey, the world's most popular free online survey service: https://www.surveymonkey.com/.*

Why Is There So Much Research Involved in Marketing?

One thing we didn't realize when we got into marketing is how much research is involved. Our account management and strategy interns are equally surprised to learn that a lot of what we do is finding information and understanding of people, places, and things.

There are the more obvious types of research such as market research and data analytics—which we've addressed in this chapter —and there is also all of the foundational research, that is essential to marketing. Effective marketing is built on understanding, and understanding is gained through research and knowledge.

Subjective Marketing

When you rely on your own bias in marketing without conducting proper research, it's often referred to as "subjective marketing"
or "personal-bias marketing." This can lead to a skewed understanding of your target audience and may result in marketing
strategies that are not effectively aligned with the needs and preferences of your customer base. Research- and data-driven insights
are crucial to developing more objective and successful marketing
campaigns.

Because you are not the consumer, it's extremely difficult for
marketers to understand the consumer pain points and motivators
without doing research. Casual observations tend to be skewed.
They are rarely grounded in reality because they come from your
personal experiences, your unique perspective, and therefore, your
biased viewpoint.

For example, in the lottery business, it is typical for marketers
to conclude that more poor people buy lottery tickets. In fact, the
data show that consumers of lottery products tend to mirror that
of the demographics of the state or jurisdiction in which tickets are
sold. It may be true that a higher percentage of lottery purchases
are made by people with lower incomes and that those purchases
represent a higher percentage of their disposable income, but the
context of those conclusions is based on the makeup of the state
demographics. It is a bias and misperception to say that the lottery
appeals only to poor people. Rather, people in all income brack-
ets and demographic groups find the appeal of winning the lottery
desirable. In actuality, the risk-reward equation factor is appealing
to people, meaning the cost of a ticket is small in relation to the
amount that could be won. Many people are willing to risk $1 for
the chance to win many thousands or, millions more, which makes
a lot of sense when you think about it that way.

AHA!

The "market landscape" refers to the overall view of the market environment in which your company operates, meaning where you plan to sell your products or services. It includes various factors that influence the industry and the people in it.

Market Landscape

One of the most essential things for you to understand is the market landscape. A "market landscape" refers to the overall view of a particular market, such as key players, trends, opportunities, challenges, and other relevant factors. It provides a comprehensive understanding of the competitive environment, customer preferences, regulatory influences, technological advancements, and economic conditions within the market.

Here are some easy ways you can go about understanding the market:

- **Industry:** Attend industry events, read industry publications, and follow social media channels.

- **Competition:** Visit the competition, try its products, and experience the purchase process.

- **Consumers:** Study their behavior firsthand. Talk to people. Watch people shopping in stores, interacting with products or patronizing venues. Pay attention to what they post on social media.

- **Trends and innovations:** Read and follow publications like *Fast Company* and *Wired*. If you watch news channels like CNN or Fox News, complement your sources of information by extending outside of your comfort zone.

Being Resourceful

You likely have a lot more resources available than you think; become more resourceful. Consider these items when conducting research.

1. THE WEB

We cannot stress enough the wealth of information available at your fingertips thanks to the internet. If you want to find out more about consumers, the industry, or the market landscape, a lot of that information is available just by searching for the right information or accessing the right sources. Some sources of information are:

- Census data
- Trade organizations
- Wikipedia
- Blogs
- *The World Almanac*
- Artificial intelligence

How you search is important when it comes to finding information online. Just about anyone can find a source to justify a point of view. Ensure you don't lead the witness, so to speak. Be open-minded, and let the information come to you. You may be pleasantly surprised by what you find.

2. UNDERSTANDING THE COMPETITION

First of all, you can't necessarily assume the competition knows what it's doing, but understanding what it's focusing on can help you see where you fit in, find out where the gaps are, and determine what opportunities have not yet been identified. When you collect the information to better understand the competition, that's called conducting a "competitive analysis."

Easy Competitive Analysis

To conduct a competitive analysis, start by listing the businesses that you would consider competition, and then go online, and look at their websites. Note the following:

- ☐ *Imagery*
- ☐ *Language and phrases*
- ☐ *Primary claims*
- ☐ *Call to action, which is text that is meant to motivate the reader to take a particular action*
- ☐ *How well they address consumer needs*
- ☐ *How well they solve the problem for the consumer*

Once you've done an assessment, find the themes that are consistent, and note the things that stand out as being clear differentiators. You can learn a lot just by looking at what everyone else is doing. Does it all look the same, or are there businesses that stand out? Chances are, the businesses that stand out have a clear brand identity and message; they consistently deliver their brand and message.

In most cases, you will discover that competitors are saying and doing the same thing. This is your opportunity to identify opportunities where you can stand out.

WARNING

Be careful not to ask leading questions when interviewing customers. Instead, leave questions open-ended.

3. EASY WAYS TO FIND OUT WHAT PEOPLE THINK

The easiest way to find out what people think is to ask them. Some examples are:

- **Customer feedback:** Track customer feedback online through social channels and networking forums like Nextdoor.

- **Facebook surveys:** Use Facebook to easily refine the audience, distribute the survey, and collect the responses.

- **Customer surveys:** Create a method for collecting customer feedback after they've made a purchase, interacted with your business, or used your services.

- **Man-on-the-street interviews:** This is an old trick of the trade otherwise known as "customer intercepts." Sure, you can hire a research firm to do this, but you can also do it yourself. Go to places where the people you want to talk to are, and kindly ask them if they wouldn't mind answering a few questions in a survey you're conducting. You can find people who are happy to share their opinions. If you take pictures or video, be sure to get their consent ahead of time.

- **Friends and family interviews:** While we recommend taking this approach with a grain of salt, it does provide an opportunity to obtain an outsider's viewpoint.

WORKSHEET

CUSTOMER-SURVEY STARTER

....

Subject: *We Value Your Opinion!*
Take Our Quick Survey, and Help Us Improve!

Dear [Customer Name],

We hope this message finds you well and you enjoyed your [visit/ stay/product]! At [Your Company Name], we are constantly striving to enhance our [products/services] to better meet your needs. Your feedback is very valuable to us, and we would greatly appreciate a few minutes of your time to complete our short survey.

Survey Link: [Insert Survey Link]

Your Opinion Matters!

Your insights will help us understand what we're doing well and identify areas where we can make improvements. The survey covers topics such as:

1. Your overall satisfaction with our [product/service]
2. Specific features you love or suggestions for improvement
3. Your preferred communication channels
4. Any additional comments or suggestions you'd like to share

How to Participate:

Simply click on the survey link above, and share your thoughts. It should only take about [estimated time] to complete.

As a Token of Our Appreciation:

As a "thank you" for your time, [mention any incentives, if applicable, such as a discount on the next purchase or entry into a giveaway].

Your feedback is instrumental in helping us serve you better. Thank you for being a valued member of the [Your Company Name] community!

Best regards,

[Your Name]
[Your Title]
[Your Contact Information]

....

Using this framework, you can customize the survey to your business. The key is to make it clear and simple while expressing your gratitude for them taking the time to share their feedback.

Surveys are also a great way to collect consumer data and build your database so you can continue to engage and communicate with your customers.

---

4. CUSTOMER JOURNEY MAP

A customer journey is the complete experience a customer has with a brand, product, or service, from initial awareness through purchase and postpurchase interactions. It involves multiple touchpoints, including awareness, consideration, purchase, retention, and advocacy.

Understanding the customer journey helps businesses tailor their strategies to meet customer needs and enhance overall satisfaction at each stage of the interaction.

An easy way to map the customer journey for your business is to mentally walk through the process of buying, from learning about the product or services, to buying, or visiting and rebuying and revisiting. Ensure your interactions with customers make sense every step of the way.

5. CONSUMER AND CULTURAL TRENDS

Staying engaged and remaining relevant is as easy as Google. Searching for information is a great way to find it. Try searching within the industry, the market, or the geography you operate in. Try searching consumer trends and areas of pop culture. Diversify your news sources. If you watch CNN, try watching Fox News. If you follow *People* magazine, check out *USA Today*. If you like Facebook, try TikTok.

> **WARNING**
>
> *When asking for customer feedback, don't ask too many questions. Limit your questions to five or fewer.*

From Research to Results

Now that you have the information, it's time to use the insights to formulate conclusions and key takeaways. This information can be used to implement changes or direct your marketing channels and messaging based on what the customer has told you he or she wants, how they felt their experience was, and what's important to them. Businesses use this information to:

- Design better products
- Improve the user experience
- Adjust sales channels
- Engage customers at different points
- Craft a marketing strategy for better results

Without market research, it's impossible to understand your customers. Use the data and research together. Data tell you "what," and research tells you "why." Without this information, you're merely making educated guesses. You may be surprised by what your customers actually think and have to say. Having the right information takes the guesswork out of planning and makes your marketing efforts more effective.

In Summary

✓ *Research, data, and insights are gold for marketers.*

✓ *Analyze your information, and create actionable steps to drive better results.*

✓ *Decide what you want to know before deciding what to ask.*

✓ *Approach information from a neutral perspective, removing personal biases.*

4

BRANDING

As with other aspects of marketing, branding may seem daunting. Branding can feel like it's reserved only for people, products, and services with megabudgets. That's simply not true. Branding can be simple; however, building and maintaining a brand requires intelligence and consistency.

CLARITY

A brand is a promise you make to the consumer so that they know what to expect.

The first thing to consider is what a brand is and what it is not.

A brand is more than a name, logo, identity, product, or price tag. It's also more than marketing and advertising. We should also mention that "brand" can sometimes be used in other ways. Sometimes, a brand is a name used to represent the company itself, what the company represents, or what the consumer believes. For example, rather than saying, "The company has done such and such," you may hear a reference to "the brand has done this and that."

Ultimately, a brand is the feeling that it evokes. That's why there are many components that make up a brand. It has secret ingredients, all carefully measured to create a unique outcome. And that brand representation is usually made up of a distinctive symbol, name, term, design, or combination thereof that represents a product, service, or company. It serves to distinguish offerings from competitors and convey values or attributes associated with the entity it represents. It's both consistent and recognizable.

The expression of a brand—how it lives in the consumer world—is what people identify and connect with. Brand identification and brand association enable people to be a part of a community of shared values and to show other people the community with which they identify.

The inner workings of a brand are the brand's value, which extends beyond tangible assets to include things like reputation, customer perception, and loyalty. This combination is a magical part of a brand—its consumer currency. A strong brand maintains a high level of consumer currency, which means it can command premium prices, foster customer trust, and differentiate itself in the marketplace. Trust goes a long way in earning and maintaining customers, even when a brand makes a mistake. Some marketers even say trust is the ultimate brand currency.

Essentially, a brand is the sum of how a product or service is perceived by consumers. The best way to look at it is from the consumer point of view, because after all, a brand exists in the mind of the consumer. Branding is simply the process of shaping consumer perceptions, and we do that by delivering the brand in a way that is both aspirational and authentic.

The Brand Pyramid

A brand pyramid is a strategic tool used in marketing to define and visualize a brand's positioning and hierarchy of attributes. It starts with the more functional benefits at the base of the pyramid and ladders up to the more aspirational and emotional aspects at the top, like the brand pyramid on the following page.
:

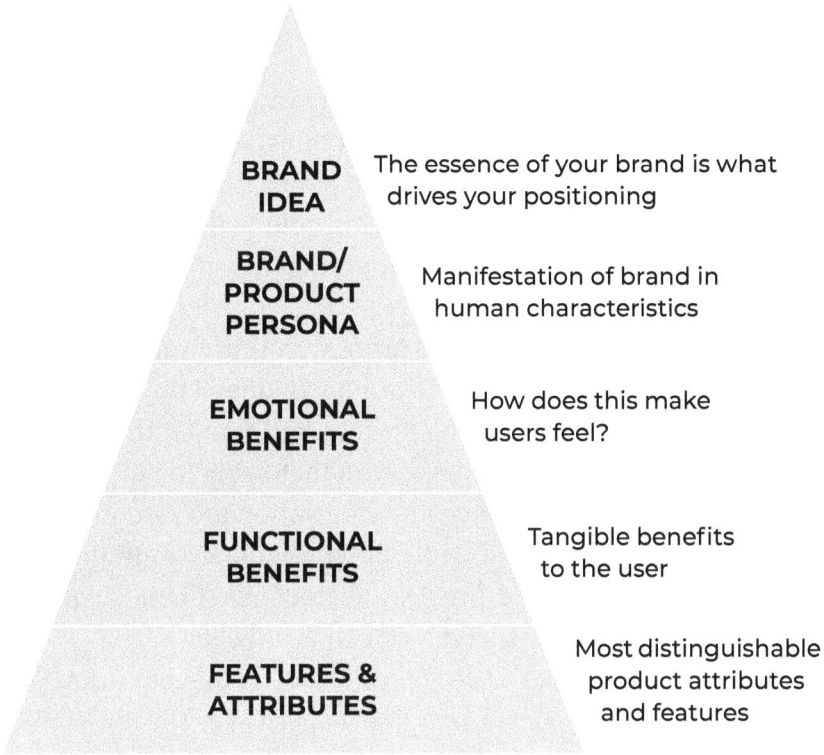

The essence of your brand is what drives your positioning — **BRAND IDEA**

Manifestation of brand in human characteristics — **BRAND/ PRODUCT PERSONA**

How does this make users feel? — **EMOTIONAL BENEFITS**

Tangible benefits to the user — **FUNCTIONAL BENEFITS**

Most distinguishable product attributes and features — **FEATURES & ATTRIBUTES**

Each layer builds on the previous one to form a pyramid. It helps companies organize the ingredients of a brand in a relative and meaningful way.

A Brand-Marketing Approach

Some companies push products by touting features and attributes, while other companies take a brand-marketing approach. These organizations treat everything they do as a brand so that consumers have a consistent experience through every touchpoint in the journey. This way, whenever anyone engages with the organization, its products, or services, that person has a consistent experience that ladders up to a set of core values.

A great example of this is Disney.

Disney

Disney utilizes a comprehensive brand-marketing approach, leveraging storytelling, emotional connections, and cross-platform integration. In its products and at its locations, it focuses on creating magical experiences, fostering nostalgia, and maintaining a consistent brand image across movies, theme parks, merchandise, and media networks.

Disney's brand ethos revolves around the core values of magic, storytelling, and imagination. Nothing it does strays from that premise. If Disney did, it wouldn't feel "on brand." The company aims to create enchanting experiences that bring joy to audiences of all ages. Integrity, creativity, and innovation are essential ingredients to the Disney brand while emphasizing a commitment to quality entertainment and timeless characters. When it comes to experiencing the Disney brand, you can just feel it.

What makes an experience you can "feel" is the many details all coming together in a single seamless experience. Disney achieves this through:

- **Attention to detail:** In Disney's parks, every detail—from the trash cans integrated into certain areas of the park to the architecture that creates immersive environments to the landscaping and wayfinding that transport guests to different worlds—is designed with an experience in mind.

- **Cast members:** Disney employees are cast members who are specifically trained to provide exceptional service and stay "in character," adding to the immersive experience.

- **Storytelling:** Every attraction at the Disney parks is carefully crafted to tell a story. The rides, shopping, dining, hotel stay, and even shuttle from the parking lot all follow a narrative that builds and maintains the storytelling aspect of the environment.

- **Waiting in line:** Yep, even waiting in line becomes part of the experience and part of the storyline using music, interactive features, and visuals.

- **Technology:** Systems like FastPass utilize technology to shorten the wait time and enhance the experience. The company's MagicBands serve as the all-in-one tool for guests to access the experience, from room key to park ticket to payment method.

- **Consistency:** Disney checks that box too! Consistency of the experience ensures that guests know what to expect. Expectation enhances satisfaction, and enhanced satisfaction improves brand perception, leading to increased trust and ultimately a greater sense of loyalty.

The seamless details are the magic of Disney.

PRO TIP

Keep even the simplest of things consistent. At Tiffany & Co., employees tie the white bow on the famous Tiffany Blue Boxes the exact same way—EVERY time.

Branding vs. Marketing

Let's address branding versus marketing. Marketing is the stuff you do to sell products and services. Take that up a notch, and there's brand marketing: a strategic approach that focuses on promoting and building a brand's identity, image, and value. It starts at the highest level of defining what it is and what it stands for. The following chart helps distinguish branding from marketing.

Branding	Marketing
Why	How
Long term	Short term
Big picture	Detailed picture
Defines vision	Defines tactics
Generates loyalty	Generates response
Creates value	Adds value
The essence of being	The act of doing

The goal of branding is to define brand purpose, establish a strong connection with the target audience, enhance brand awareness, and differentiate the brand from competitors in the market. When you have a strong sense of what your brand stands for and what it delivers to the consumer, then you can create a bond that lasts beyond a purchase transaction. And when you take a brand-marketing approach, you've created a strategy from which marketing activities can operate.

From Brand Loyalty to Brand Affinity

Brand loyalty is a wonderful thing. It refers to the tendency of consumers to consistently choose one brand over another. Yet it goes beyond simple repeat purchases and usually involves a deeper emotional connection. The kind of connection that makes someone "loyal" to your brand. Someone loyal to your brand is likely to choose it without considering another option. Brand-loyal customers are likelier to continue buying products or services from the same brand, even when faced with alternative options with better added perks or at a lower price. Building and maintaining loyalty often involves delivering consistent quality, positive experiences, and effective communication consistently.

Let's discuss effective examples of brand affinity to better understand the difference between loyalty and affinity.

Harley-Davidson

Known for its community of loyal followers, Harley-Davidson's brand affinity is built on a combination of heritage, style, community, marketing, customization, distinctive features, and a global presence that collectively creates a strong emotional connection with its audience.

But how does Harley create this level of brand affinity? Well, there are many factors that contribute to this level of brand affinity:

- **Heritage and tradition:** Its history dates back to the early 20th century. History alone doesn't create this level of affinity, but leveraging its heritage and tradition in a meaningful way to consumers does. Harley does this by creating a sense of nostalgia and authenticity that appeals to riders.

- **Distinctive design and style:** Harley motorcycles are known for their iconic design and distinctive style. The company has maintained a consistent aesthetic. There's that word again: "consistent."

- **Community and brotherhood:** You don't have to be a motorcycle enthusiast to recognize the fact that Harley has cultivated a strong sense of community among its riders. The Harley Owners Group (HOG) is a great example of how a brand has provided a platform for Harley enthusiasts to connect, share experiences, and participate.

- **Lifestyle marketing:** The brand's marketing efforts go well beyond selling motorcycles; they promote a lifestyle that is synonymous with freedom, adventure, and a rebellious spirit. Through advertising, hosting events, and collaborations, the brand reinforces this lifestyle image.

- **Personalization:** Harley riders often customize their bikes to reflect their individuality. The brand also encourages customization to enables riders to create their own riding experience, thereby fostering an even deeper relationship between the rider and the brand.

- **Merchandise:** The company's iconic logo and lifestyle branding have extended beyond motorcycles to include apparel, accessories, and collectibles.

- **Sound:** Brands aren't just visual. The distinctive sound of a Harley is a key element of its identity. The deep rumble of the engine is instantly recognizable and adds to the overall experience of riding a Harley.

- **Global reach:** Harley has a global presence, and its motorcycles are recognized around the world. This global appeal helps in creating a sense of belonging, regardless of where you are in the world.

- **Brand loyalty:** It's no surprise that loyalty is an element of the affinity Harley has created among its audience. The brand has successfully maintained a dedicated customer base for more than 120 years.

Loyalty and affinity both represent a relationship with a customer. How they differ is how they deliver to the customer. You could say that loyalty is a component of affinity and that affinity is at the deepest level of brand engagement.

Here is a chart that very simply illustrates the nuances between the two relationships.

Brand Loyalty	Brand Affinity
Provides value	Shares value
Rational response	Emotional reasoning
Behavior	Feeling
Maintenance	Enduring
Deep level of relationship	Deepest level of relationship

A Lifestyle Brand

In the Harley-Davidson example, we mentioned this idea of a lifestyle brand; this is also true of Disney. A lifestyle brand is one that embodies the values, aspirations, interests, attitudes, and opinions of a group of people for marketing purposes. These brands seek to inspire, guide, and motivate. A lifestyle brand becomes something that people relate to on a personal level, aligns with their way of life, and defines them. The brand is something people want to be a part of on a deeper level because it tells a story.

AHA!
Henry Ford famously said, "You can't build up a reputation on what you are going to do."

Personal Branding

This brings us to the ever-popular topic of personal branding. If you are a business owner or entrepreneur, you may be interested in understanding more about how your personal brand interacts with your business, product, service, or organizational brand.

CLARITY

There really isn't a separation between a personal life and a professional life anymore. This is why it's important to ensure that people's experience when they meet you matches their expectations.

If you're wondering what a business brand has to do with a personal brand, one has everything to do with the other. Whether personal or business, a brand essentially means the same thing. It's an authentic manifestation of who you are, what you do, how you do it, and who you serve.

Business brands and personal brands are both made up of the same essential ingredients, although how they express themselves may differ. Think of the ingredients as the convergence of these four elements:

1. A past with existing equities—a history that makes up the existing perception

2. Plans and aspirations for the future—the vision for the future

3. A dynamic world in which the brand must survive and prevail, also known as the "competitive landscape"

4. People whom it must please, or the "constituent resonance"

Depending on the life of the brand, it may have more or less of a past. For example, a new brand may have less equity and more vision.

COMPANY	CULTURE
Keep existing brand equities	Have a vision for the future to accommodate change
CORE BRAND STRATEGY	
CONSUMER	CATEGORY
Satisfy emotional needs	Stand out in a competitive landscape

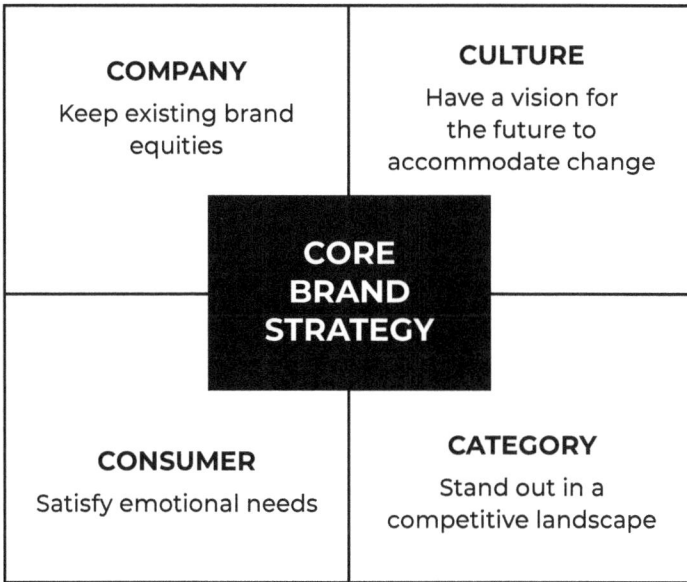

Branding Is Art + Science

It's important to emphasize that branding is not a one-way street of touting product attributes and selling product benefits. Branding is tapping into the psychology of human behavior to create emotional currency. This emotion may not come naturally, as the natural instinct is "convince me that I need this and why I need it," and a brand tells you "what this means to me" or what it delivers—emotionally, not necessarily rationally. Remember—people make decisions based on emotion or how it makes them feel.

We like to think of brands as a balance of art and science. The science is what goes into creating and defining a brand, which we call the "emotional ingredients." The art is how the brand communicates, or how it's brought to life. It's the expression or application of a brand. A brand doesn't really exist unless it's expressed. A logo or a story sitting on a shelf isn't much of a brand until it's been given the opportunity to interact with people.

When it comes to personal brands, the most effective personal brand tells us who a person is and where his or her expertise lies. A personal brand may include elements such as:

- Specific knowledge of an industry or topic
- Unique point of view or approach
- Unique and authentic personality

Just as a company and its products must have values that align, a person and his or her product or service offering must have values that align. Some of the best examples of people who have strong personal brands are considered personal brand mavericks. These people lead by example; it won't take much convincing for you to understand why they are so aligned with their business ventures. Here are some of our favorite real-life examples when it comes to personal brands and the companies they represent.

Richard Branson

You may recognize Sir Richard Branson and his Virgin brands. The Virgin companies range from entertainment and health to wellness, money, people, planet technology, and the travel and leisure space. Virgin brands like Virgin Atlantic, Virgin Money, Virgin Wines, and Virgin Hotels all have one thing in common: Richard Branson. Branson has created a brand built on innovation and disruption based on his personal branding mantra, "Screw it, let's do it."

Everything about him embodies his free-spirited, love-for-life approach to life and business. Have you ever noticed that when you see a picture of Branson, the top button (or two) on his shirt is always unbuttoned, making him look relaxed, his hair slightly unruly as if he's in a tropical breeze, and his gaze is into some faraway place? All of this is consistent with his personality and his personal brand. You know exactly what to expect from Branson—consistently.

Why his personal brand works:

- It embodies his spirit of adventure.

- He is a champion for innovation and disruption.

- His actions match his words.

- He inspires while having fun.

AHA!

Add to your reading list some titles written by Sir Richard Branson, and learn firsthand about what it means to build a corporate brand from a personal brand.

- *Screw It, Let's Do It: Lessons in Life and Business*
- *Like a Virgin: Secrets They Won't Teach You at Business School*
- *The Virgin Way: Everything I Know About Leadership*

Oprah

Then there's Oprah Winfrey. We all know her simply as "Oprah." A funny story about Oprah and her personal brand is that she famously rejected the idea of being a brand—which is in itself part of her brand. She has stated on multiple occasions that she is a person, not a brand, fearing she would lose the rare connection she had with her audience. Later, she realized that she was the brand. "I was once afraid of people saying, 'Who does she think she is?', and now I have the courage to say, 'This is who I am.'"

Oprah has a brand built on empathy and storytelling. No matter what she does in entertainment, on screen or off, she is true to her personal brand mantra: Surround yourself only with people who lift you higher.

Why her personal brand works:

- We know her as "Oprah."

- She's living her dream life—and being paid for it.

- She uses her branding to change people's actions—
for the better.

- She embodies a strong spirit of giving.

 AHA!
A simple gut check when considering a brand extension or application is to ask yourself, "Is this on brand?"

Today's Rules for Building a Personal Brand

We could tell you what you need to do to create an effective brand, but sometimes it's easier to get the point across with mistakes people make when it comes to branding. Here are seven common mistakes, why they are mistakes, and what you can do instead—the rules.

Mistake #1: **Not defining your brand identity**	*Rule #1:* **Clearly define your genuine values**
This can confuse people, and they may not know what to expect.	Define who you are, what you do, and how you do it.
Mistake #2: **Not differentiating**	*Rule #2:* **Create a competitive advantage**
This doesn't mean being louder; it means standing out from the crowd.	Define what you do that no one else can or what you can do better than anyone else.

Mistake #3: **Not knowing your audience**	*Rule #3:* **Understand your audience**
You can't be all things to all people. If you try, you will be nothing to everyone.	Identify the kind of people you resonate with, and focus on them.
Mistake #4: **Not creating valuable content**	*Rule #4:* **Lean into storytelling and problem-solving**
A brand that isn't expressed doesn't exist.	Create content to bring your brand to life.
Mistake #5: **Not leveraging social media**	*Rule #5:* **Focus on quality, not quantity**
It's powerful and cost-effective.	Create content to engage your audience.
Mistake #6: **Not being consistent**	*Rule #6:* **Follow your North Star**
When you're inconsistent, people won't know what to expect from you.	Follow your guiding light, and stick to your core values. Ensure that your actions match your words, consistently.
Mistake #7: **Not tracking**	*Rule #7:* **Listen and evaluate often**
You can't improve what you don't measure.	Don't be afraid to seek feedback, learn from what people have to say, and implement changes. This is a way to constantly improve yourself.

ACTIVITY: PERSONAL-BRAND WORKSHEET

ACHIEVING OPTIMAL BRAND POTENTIAL

Personal-branding is the story people tell about you when you're not in the room.

INGREDIENTS FOR BUILDING A PERSONAL BRAND

Focused

Determine what you want to be known for—be specific and memorable. Make sure it is grounded in truth.

Targeted

Define the audience and community.
Who do you resonate with?

Expert and Amplification

Tell your story—create an online presence through content marketing. Pay attention to the tone.

YOUR BRAND ELEMENTS

What you do

The value delivered

For whom you do work

The idea audience

How you do it

The unique selling proposition that sets you apart from everyone else

CREATE YOUR BRAND STATEMENT

Use the brand elements to create one or two sentences that sum up your brand.

MISSION

Practical: Describe why you exist.

VISION

Visionary: Describe your long-term goal.

THE CHECKLIST FOR SUCCESS

Rules for building a personal brand:

- ☐ Clearly define: brand statement
- ☐ Be different from everyone else: competitive advantage
- ☐ Know your audience: definition of the audience
- ☐ Bring your brand to life: creation of the story
- ☐ Engage on social media: active engagement with your audience
- ☐ Be consistent: staying the course—on and offline
- ☐ Evaluate and refine: keep continued evolution

Action Plan

Now that you know the mistakes and have learned the rules for creating and maintaining an effective brand, let's recap what you can do by way of an action plan. Staying mindful of these elements —whether a business brand, personal brand, or both—will ensure greater success:

- Be clear about who you are.
- Differentiate with an advantage.
- Focus on the people who matter.
- Deliver value.
- Engage with people in ways that are meaningful to them.
- Make the experience consistent.
- Listen, and grow.

Brand Architecture

Part of your brand strategy is what is known as "brand architecture." This is the hierarchy of brands, or sub-brands branded products, and extensions within an organization. The goal of a brand architecture is to make sense of the pieces and to provide a primary brand platform where all the parts can exist as part of a brand strategy.

Brand architecture is basically a technique for providing structure for how the parts relate to one another. It's a way of organizing many things within one company or under a single brand. These structures are meant to provide room for growth. So whether you expand wide or deep in your offerings, the organization of the parts and their relationship to each other make sense.

Let's say that you have a real estate development company and you also create content through a blog, a book, and a seminar. The company may be your primary branded offering, and the content pieces are extensions that must fit within your overarching brand.

Types of brand architecture and examples from familiar brands follow.

Brand Models

When it comes to choosing the right model for your brand, there is no right or wrong answer. It depends on whatever works best for you—now and in the future. You may consider what model provides the best path for growth and expansion of your business.

The basic models for brand architecture are:

- **Branded house:** In a branded house, the master brand and sub-brands have the same identity with some variations. For example, Apple uses name extensions under the "Apple" moniker, and FedEx uses different colors for each of its business divisions.

- **Endorsed brands:** When it comes to endorsed brands, the master brand supports sub-brands with unique designs within the same family of brands—let's say they share the same DNA but are not exactly the same. For example, Nestle endorses Kit Kat and Crunch, both in the candy category.

- **House of brands:** In a house of brands, there is no linkage between the sub-brands or products. Each brand has a totally unique identity and the strength to stand on its own. The best example of this is Procter & Gamble. Brands within its portfolio include Pampers, Tide, Charmin, Bounty, Gillette, Old Spice, Cascade, and Tampax. And that's only a few examples.

- **Hybrid-brand model:** The hybrid model uses a mix of approaches. It usually starts out with one brand, but through branded extensions and/or acquisitions of new brands, it takes on a hybrid structure. Coca-Cola is an example of a hybrid brand. It has Coke products, along with many individually branded products with unique identities.

Here are examples of famous brands to help you visualize the options.

BRAND ARCHITECTURE EXAMPLES

Branded House

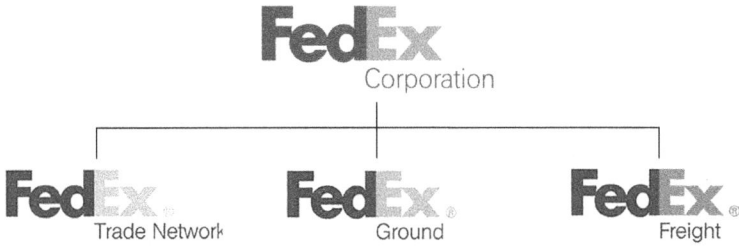

Endorsed Brands

House of Brands

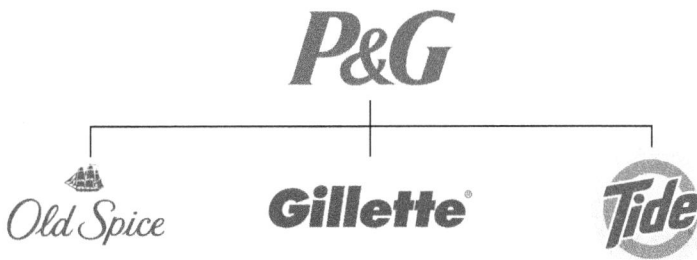

That's as far as we're going to get into brand architecture. Having a basic understanding of the structures and how they work provides a good foundation for you as you approach your own brand planning. Thinking about the structure in advance helps so that you avoid ending up with a bunch of disparate elements that don't relate and have difficulty working together. Enabling brands to work together creates awareness, cultivates familiarity, and breeds trust.

Branding and How to Deliver Your Brand

Building a strong brand involves delivering a consistent and compelling message to your target audience through various channels, and there are many ways to do this. An effective brand initiative means generating consistency and awareness in support of more specific products and services. Let's touch on some of the more common key delivery methods for branding. These are the methods in which your brand is expressed to the people who buy what you're selling.

- **Logo and visual identity:** Create the visual elements that represent your brand and are used for identification. They should be simple, easy to read, and memorable, with the ability to adapt to a variety of applications, large and small.

....

SENSORY BRANDING

Something interesting to consider is that a visual identity may also be complemented by other sensory elements such as scent.

The Westin hotel chain rolled out its signature White Tea scent and a line of amenities more than a decade ago, aiming to energize guests with the blend of white tea, wood cedar, and vanilla. So when you walk into a Westin, the scent becomes part of the sensory experience and, thus, a contributing factor to the brand experience, transporting the guest by fragrance.

Another way to approach a sensory-branded experience is through audio identification. "Intel inside" is a good example of an audio tag used in advertising to identify products that contain Intel components. The "Intel inside" audio tag is a brief jingle or sound logo. It's often heard in commercials and promotional materials for computers and other devices featuring Intel processors in order to identify the "ingredient brand" for consumers.

And yet another way to approach a brand is by food—for example: the scent of a freshly baked chocolate chip cookie. Among the many signature things that DoubleTree by Hilton is known for are its chocolate chip cookies. They were originally made in the early 1980s for VIPs, but they're now given to all guests and have been made by Nashville-based Christie Cookie Co. for more than 30 years. This signature element is used to create a distinguished sense of arrival and a unique welcome.

In 2020, during the COVID-19 pandemic, the brand published an e-adapted recipe for its cookies to maintain top-of-mind relevance with consumers during a time when travel was suspended.

- **Messaging:** Craft a clear and compelling message that communicates your unique value proposition. You may use elements from your business plan and create messaging for your pitch deck and advertising as a way to differentiate your brand from the competition.

- **Content marketing:** Create high-quality and relevant content for use in blogs, articles, videos, social posts, on your website, and other content formats to engage your audience.

- **Social media:** Establish a strong presence on the channels most relevant to your target audience.

E-FYI

Just because a social media channel exists, it doesn't mean it's right for you. Choose the channels your audience frequents.

- **Website:** This is the most essential foundational element for your business and your brand. Your website reflects your brand and delivers a positive user experience.

- **Advertising:** Develop creative, relevant, and impactful campaigns across a variety of channels.

- **Packaging and product design:** Every touchpoint must align with your brand. Design packaging and products that reflect your brand identity. The physical presentation of your products helps contribute to brand recognition and recall.

- **Public relations:** Build relationships with media outlets, and provide them with news to secure positive coverage.

- **Customer experience:** Whether it's B2B or B2C, your business is likely interacting with people. Make your customer experience the best it can be to build positive associations with your brand and lasting relationships.

- **Team members:** Employees are such an essential part of your business. Communicate with your employees. Take the time to confirm your employees understand and embody your brand values. Train them to be brand ambassadors who advocate for your brand.

- **Sponsorships and partnerships:** We'll discuss this topic in more detail in Chapter 10. It's important to ensure that your brand associations make sense and that they are in alignment with what you stand for. Form partnerships that are mutually beneficial, enhance your brand image, and help yourself reach new audiences. This includes everything from events to sponsorships to community engagement.

It's important to remember that when it comes to branding, every touchpoint matters, and consistency is essential. That's why you consistently hear us mention consistency.

Now that we have identified the brand, what it stands for, and the ways in which it's expressed to consumers, let's talk about brand guidelines—the rules guiding the brand in your marketing and communications.

Brand Guidelines

We said that a brand doesn't exist unless it is expressed, meaning it's brought to life and interacts with people. To manage the process, you may want to create brand guidelines as the rules the brand lives by in all communications and forms of expression. The brand guidelines typically include the following elements:

- **Brand identity:** Outline of the brand's mission, vision, values, and personality traits.

- **Logo usage:** Guidelines for logo variations, sizes, clear space, and acceptable color variations. It may also include what not to do.

- **Typography:** Specifications for fonts used in branding and visual communications, including primary and secondary typefaces, sizes, and usage instructions.

- **Color palette:** Detailed information about the brand's color scheme, including primary and secondary colors, as well as guidelines for color usage in various contexts.

- **Imagery and photography:** Guidance on the style, tone, and types of images that align with the brand's visual identity. This may include examples.

- **Layout and design:** Instructions on how to create visually consistent materials, including guidelines for layouts, grids, and design elements.

- **Voice and tone:** Recommendations for the brand's communication style, including preferred language, tone, and messaging guidelines. Some brands may take a more fun approach than others. Some may use humor, while others are more matter-of-fact.

- **Usage examples:** Examples of properly and improperly executed brand elements, demonstrating correct usage in various contexts.

- **Brand application:** Guidelines or templates for applying the brand across different media, such as print, digital, signage, and merchandise.

- **Legal considerations:** Information regarding trademark usage, copyright permissions, and any other legal considerations.

These are the things you should consider when developing your brand, and many of the elements in the brand guidelines may also be found in the business plan, pitch deck, or investor presentation and repurposed. It's also important to update and maintain the brand guidelines to ensure consistency and relevance over time, as it's not unusual for brands to evolve or to expand or for there to be a need for a new application.

If you outsource your communications materials to a graphic designer or media outlet to execute creative assets, you can provide the brand guidelines to give thst party the information it needs. It's also a good idea to have a package of the brand assets you can share with your partners. The brand assets may include things like downloadable files for logos, fonts, colors, and other assets for use by internal and external stakeholders.

When it comes to developing the guidelines for your brand, it can be as comprehensive or simple as you would like it to be. In fact, a brand-guidelines document can be a single page.

AHA!

According to McKinsey & Company, "Future-ready companies share these characteristics—they know who they are and what they stand for."

....

In Summary

✓ *A brand tells people what they can expect.*

✓ *Some elements that may be used to represent a brand are name, logo, tagline, color scheme, or even a scent.*

✓ *Business brands and personal brands are made up of the same ingredients.*

✓ *A brand does not exist unless it is expressed in a way that engages with people.*

✓ *A good way to gut-check branding is to simply ask yourself, "Is this on brand?"*

....

5

THE MARKETING
PLAN

Planning is crucial, because it helps you set clear goals, prioritize tasks, allocate resources, and anticipate potential issues. It's like creating a road map that guides you toward your desired destination in both personal and professional endeavors. We think you'll agree that people who plan are the ones who get things done and who can celebrate accomplishments. They make it to the finish line.

This chapter is dedicated to creating a marketing plan, including developing the most cost-effective marketing strategy for your business and determining the best way to measure the success of your marketing campaigns.

CLARITY
A marketing plan provides a road map for achieving your business goals and objectives. Without one, you're wandering aimlessly through a complicated consumer landscape.

Simply stated, a marketing plan is a comprehensive plan for marketing efforts and typically includes strategies, tactics, markets, and messaging. A marketing plan supports your business goals and consists of strategies and tactics to help you drive revenue.

Before we get into the plan itself, let's start by addressing the budget. Starting with a budget helps define order of magnitude.

That is, framing how big or small the effort may end up being, in order to set expectations.

Determining a Marketing Budget

One of the most important parts of a marketing plan is determining a budget. While there are no real hard and fast rules, there are guidelines that may be helpful in determining a budget or affirming your existing marketing budget.

AHA!
Marketing is an investment, not an expense.

Let's start with a guideline for how much you should expect to allocate toward marketing. A marketing budget is typically a percentage of forecast revenue. It also depends on where your business or product currently stands in the cycle. For example, new brands with little to no awareness may require more advertising to create lift at launch. Conversely, more established brands with a more established level of consumer awareness may require a little less of a marketing-budget allocation. It also depends on the competition, category, and marketplace.

To keep it simple and to give you an idea of how to develop a budget, we can follow some more general guidelines. Deloitte conducted a survey providing percentage of revenue by industry as benchmark for companies to determine spend on marketing.[2]

---

2   https://blog.hubspot.com/marketing/marketing-budget-percentage

Industry	Marketing Budget (Percent of Company Revenue)
Banking, finance, insurance, real estate	8%
Communications media	10%
Consumer packaged goods	9%
Consumer services	6%
Education	3%
Energy	1%
Health care	18%
Manufacturing	13%
Mining and construction	3%
Retail wholesale	14%
Service consulting	21%
Technology	21%
Transportation	6%

Budgets are essential. They help focus your marketing efforts. Knowing exactly what you want to spend on marketing helps in the planning process and in determining where the budget will be allocated by function.

Once you have determined your marketing spend, the following chart is an easy breakdown of allocation percentage by function.

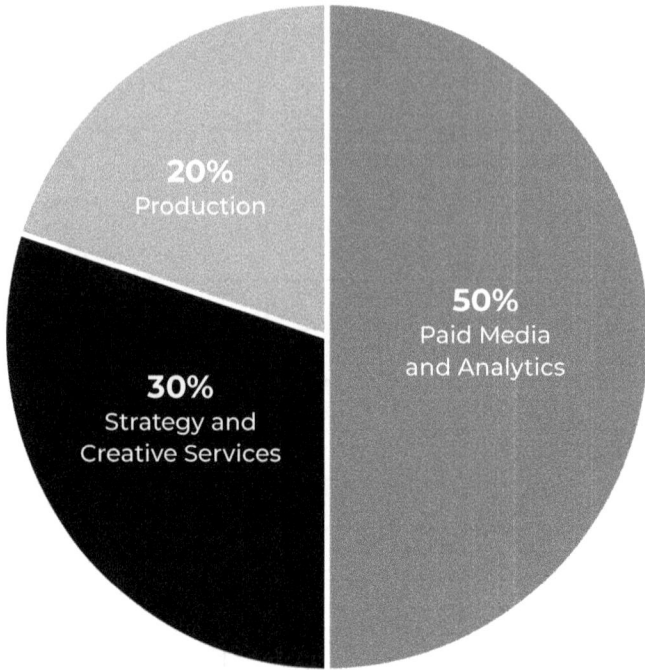

Expect to spend roughly half of your marketing budget on different forms of paid media. This includes digital advertising (such as paid digital advertising), search engine marketing, and paid social media, as well as traditional forms of marketing such as direct mail, billboards, public relations, and sponsorships.

Expect to spend about 20 percent of your marketing budget on production. This is the cost to produce the advertising assets, like photography and video production.

Expect to spend about 30 percent of your marketing budget for the marketing fees—that is the professional freelancers, designers, or consultants—to create the campaign or creative aspects of your marketing.

WORKSHEET

BUDGET-BUILDER

MARKETING BUDGET

Department name:

Prepared by:

Date created:

Date Reviewed:

Marketing/Promotion	Jan	Feb	Mar	Apr	May	June	July	Aug	Sep	Oct	Nov	Dec
Marketing agency	1049.00											
Radio advertising												
TV advertising				270.00								
Print advertising												
Online advertising												
Social media	133.00											
SEO			300.00									
Mail-outs		500.00										
Giveaways												
Events												
Artwork												
Merchandising												
Publications												
TOTAL	1182.00	500.00	300.00	270.00	0.00	0.00	0.00	0.00	0.00	0.00	0.00	0.00

Creating a Marketing Plan

While you are not necessarily a marketing professional, marketing is one of the many functions you will likely need to address as a business owner. Much like a business plan, a marketing plan is a process that can be as simple or as complicated as you want it to be. Don't put too much pressure on yourself to make it perfect. A marketing plan is meant to be an evergreen and evolving business tool to support your efforts and measure your success.

We'll walk you through the step-by-step process. You may not have all the answers, and that's okay. The most important thing is that you give these elements thought and that you approach your marketing efforts deliberately. Trust us—it will make life much easier to have a playbook to guide your decisions.

As mentioned earlier, keep in mind that some of the information from your business plan or business proposal can be repurposed for parts of the marketing plan. An example of "repurposed information" may be the business objective. Let's say your business plan states an objective of selling 500 units per quarter. To support the business goal—from the business plan—a marketing objective would get the audience to purchase 500 units. A strategy could be offering an incentive, and a tactic could be to serve digital ads on complementary products.

PRO TIP

- *Keep your plan focused and concise.*
- *Tailor your plan to your specific business and industry.*
- *Be flexible and willing to adapt your plan based on results and market changes.*
- *You don't have to do it all or do everything at once—consider a planning process in bite-size pieces.*

The Plan Itself

We will walk through the components of a marketing plan and what each section entails. You can use some of it or all of it. The most important things to have are your business goals defined and an idea of the marketing support you will use to achieve them.

- **Executive Summary**

  The executive summary is something that comes first but that you do last. The summary is a brief overview of your entire marketing plan, including key goals, strategies, tactics, and anticipated results. In order to provide a brief overview, you will need to do your plan first. It summarizes your plan and approach to marketing for your business.

- **Business Overview**

  The business overview provides an overview of what your business offers.

  In this section:

    o Define your business objectives.

    o Describe your business products/services.

    o Describe your business mission, vision, and values.

    o Identify your target market and customer demographics.

    o Highlight your unique selling proposition—what sets your business or product apart.

- **Business Analysis**

  The business analysis explores how your business compares to other businesses in the market and how it intends to compete within the marketplace.

o *Competitive Analysis*

List who you consider to be your competition, both in and out of the category. Out of the category would include businesses with products that consumers are willing to spend money on rather than buying your products/ services. For example, a smoothie shop's competition is not just other smoothie shops; it's also the quick-serve restaurants in the area.

Once you have compiled a list of competitors, do a little research so that you can better understand what they have to offer and how they are positioning themselves. Within the competitive landscape you can identify gaps—or territories—that are not yet claimed by the competition. This is also where you can identify opportunities.

WORKSHEET

Competitive Analysis

Company Name	Product	Positioning	Call to Action or Offer

- o *Market Trends*

  Market trends consist of information you likely already know as an expert in your industry, including the industry trends and other influences on consumers or the industry. This could also include external factors that may impact your business, such as economic factors, changes in technology, or distribution channels.

- **SWOT Analysis**

  You may have already cited the strengths, weaknesses, opportunities, and threats (SWOT) as part of your business plan. As a reminder, a SWOT analysis is made up of internal and external factors. Internal factors are strengths and weaknesses; external factors are opportunities and threats.

- **Target Audience**

  Chapter 2 was dedicated to this subject, because the people who buy what you're selling are that important—understanding who they are and how they make buying decisions is essential to your success. It allows you to craft the right messages and deliver them to the right people in the right channels.

  The activities in this section include:

  - o Clearly defining your target audience
  - o Identifying their needs, preferences, pain points, and behaviors
  - o Explaining how your product or service meets their needs

- **Marketing Goals and Objectives**

  It is an important distinction not to confuse marketing goals with business goals. You will have already defined your business goals as part of your business plan. The marketing goals and objectives are in support of your business goals. Outline the objectives that support each goal.

  A good way to check the validity of a marketing goal is to ask yourself, "Can marketing accomplish this?" As examples, here are some things that marketing can accomplish:

  - Increasing brand awareness
  - Driving sales
  - Building customer loyalty
  - Engaging target audiences

  Marketing can also help in market research, product positioning, and creating a positive brand image. Ultimately, effective marketing aligns with overall business goals and contributes to organizational growth.

PRO TIP

Marketing goals and objectives can be used interchangeably but must be quantifiable and, therefore, measurable.

- **Marketing Strategies**

  - *Positioning:* Describe your product or service and its unique features. Determine your pricing strategy. Determine the unique value proposition that your product and company offer.

- ○ *Channels:* Outline your distribution channels and how you will get your product to customers.

- ○ *Promotion:* Detail your promotional strategies, including advertising, public relations, and digital marketing. This may also include an acquisition strategy about what you are willing to spend to gain a customer in the way of free offers, trial offers, or related elements.

- **Marketing Tactics and Action Plan**

  - ○ *Tactics:* Specify the tactics you'll use to implement each strategy. Include details on advertising campaigns, social media plans, content marketing, etc. This would include stating exactly which media channels (TV, digital advertising, etc.) and social media platforms (Instagram, Facebook, etc.) you would use.

  - ○ *Timing:* Create a timeline to operate against, including time to produce and time to execute. Consider if there is seasonality to your business; if so, shift the offers and messaging.

- **Budget and Resource Allocation**

  Allocate a budget for each marketing tactic. Operating against a predetermined budget will help you and make choices and prioritize efforts. Above all, be realistic, and ensure your budget aligns with your overall business goals.

PRO TIP

When it comes to budgeting, be strategic about the timing of your spending. You may not want to spread it out evenly. Some marketing efforts require front-loading the investment to get traction out of the gate, and others are "flighted" (meaning scheduled in peaks to leverage seasonality or consumer buying habits).

- **Implementation Plan**
    - o Develop a timeline for the execution of each tactic.
    - o Assign responsibilities and roles within your team.
    - o Consider conducting regular check-ins to ensure tactics are on track.
- **Monitoring and Measurement**
    - o *Track efforts:* Outline how you will track and measure the success of your marketing efforts over the long term.
    - o *Analytics and measurement:* Identify key performance indicators (KPIs) for each tactic. Use data to make informed decisions in real time or over the long term in planning.

E-FYI

A great online resource for measuring advertising KPIs is Google Analytics. You can sign up for an account on the Google Analytics website, and Google offers a free version that provides basic analytics functionality.

- **Risks and Assumptions**
    - o Include any assumptions and other practical considerations that go along with the details of your plan. It can't hurt to have notes and provide context to support the elements that make up your plan.
    - o Anticipate potential problems and challenges.
    - o Outline contingency plans.
    - o Be prepared to adapt your strategies based on market changes.

- **Conclusion**

    - o Summarize key points and restate goals.

    - o Include the next step: the next time you plan to revisit and update your plan.

    - o Update to keep the plan relevant and effective.

....

CAMPAIGN MEASUREMENT

Advertising-campaign measurement is not always a straight line.

You can use tools like Google Analytics to track the effectiveness of digital campaigns and measure online conversions.

Through various research methodologies, you can measure ad recall among consumers and track brand awareness and brand perception:

- ☐ *Ad recall refers to how well people remember seeing or hearing an ad.*

- ☐ *Brand awareness measures the extent to which consumers recognize a brand.*

- ☐ *Brand perception tells you how consumers feel about a brand and whether it's positive or negative.*

Other, less scientific ways to measure advertising effectiveness include tracking your sales by the timing of your marketing efforts, media plans, and promotions. Or by website traffic, in-store foot traffic, and sales associated with the timing of ad placements and offers.

....

Managing the Marketing Plan

An essential part of the planning process is to review and update. We suggest that you even make this part of your plan. At the end of your plan, schedule time to revisit it in order to review it and update it.

A marketing plan doesn't sit on a shelf. There is no such thing as setting it and forgetting it when it comes to marketing. Marketing is an evergreen process that requires ongoing nurturing. You will learn from your mistakes and make adjustments based on responses and changing market dynamics. The consumer market is dynamic, and you must evolve and adapt to changing consumer preferences and behaviors.

We can't emphasize enough how important it is to regularly review and update your marketing plan to reflect changes in the market or in your business goals. This also offers quantifiable support to help justify your marketing investment.

PRO TIP

Plan to revisit your marketing plan goals and strategies at least annually and your objectives and tactics quarterly.

WORSHEET

Marketing-Plan Template

An abbreviated format and quick explanation of the basic outline for a marketing plan, including the purpose of each section, follows. A marketing plan can be simple, as long as it enables you to focus and measure marketing activities against the purpose.

☐ **Executive summary:** Put it first; do it last. This is a summary of your overall approach.

☐ **Business overview:** This is an overview of what your business offers.

☐ **Business analysis:** This is how your business compares to other businesses in the market and how it intends to compete within the marketplace.

☐ **SWOT analysis:** A SWOT analysis is made up of internal and external factors. Internal factors are strengths and weaknesses, and the external factors are opportunities and threats.

☐ **Target audience:** It's not everyone; it's the people likeliest to buy your products or services.

☐ **Marketing goals and objectives:** These are the marketing goals and objectives that support your business goals.

☐ **Marketing strategies:** These are the approaches that businesses use to promote and sell their products or services, aiming to reach and attract customers.

☐ **Marketing tactics and action plan:** These are that activities and timing used to implement the strategies.

☐ **Budget and resource allocation:** This is a breakdown of the overall marketing budget by allocating a budget for each marketing activity.

☐ **Implementation plan:** This comprises the activities, timing, and team responsibilities needed to activate the marketing plan.

☐ **Monitoring and measurement:** This is the tracking and measurement of the success of your marketing efforts.

☐ **Risks and assumptions:** This is anticipating problems and having contingency plans.

☐ **Review and update:** This is conducting an ongoing review and making updates to the marketing plan.

PRO TIP

Begin with the end in mind. When creating a critical path, start with the due date for the deliverable and work backward. It is essential that you meet the deadlines along the way—or negotiate within the timeline.

CLARITY

A strategy is the implementation of a simple important idea over time, not a lengthy action plan. An action plan can be used to support a strategy.

....

In Summary

✓ *A marketing plan is an essential tool that serves as a road map to guide your marketing efforts.*

✓ *A marketing plan is evergreen and should be revisited frequently and evolve as your business grows and the landscape changes.*

✓ *A marketing plan can be as simple or as comprehensive as you would like it to be.*

✓ *The most important things to have are defined business goals and an understanding of the marketing support you will use to achieve them.*

....

6

DIGITAL MARKETING

Digital marketing gets its own chapter for a few reasons. First, simply for the fact that we're living in the digital age—characterized by the widespread use of digital technology and the internet to create, share, and access information. For marketers, digital marketing can be cost-efficient and effective at creating awareness, which then can convert customers to make a purchase. Few media can cover all steps of the marketing funnel in one place. Online or on their phone, a person can literally go from awareness to consideration to conversion in one visit and a few clicks, whether you reach out to him or her directly with targeted messaging or they find you online.

It's no secret that most of us use digital platforms to buy things or obtain information. Here's how it can work for your business, selling your products and services.

Facts First

Let's begin by level-setting with some general statistics about phone and internet usage.

- **Smartphone usage:**
    - More than 3.8 billion people worldwide own smartphones.

- o On average, people spend more than three hours a day on their phones.
- o Mobile apps account for more than 90 percent of internet usage.

- **Internet usage:**
  - o Globally there are more than 4.9 billion internet users.
  - o More than 60 percent of the global population has access to the internet.
  - o Social media platforms have more than 3.6 billion active users.

- **E-commerce:**
  - o Online sales are expected to surpass $4.5 trillion globally.
  - o More than 2.1 billion people worldwide shop online.

- **Video streaming:**
  - o Video streaming constitutes a significant portion of internet traffic, with popular platforms like YouTube and Netflix.
  - o YouTube has more than 2 billion logged-in users monthly.

- **Social media:**
  - o Facebook remains the largest social media platform, with more than 2.8 billion active users.
  - o Instagram has more than 1 billion active users monthly.
  - o X has more than 330 million active users monthly.

While these statistics may vary depending on the source and time frame, the widespread usage of phones and the internet is undeniable.

Understand how it works, and plan to use digital marketing as part of your marketing plan.

What's Great about It

Digital marketing encompasses a wide range of activities with the purpose of promoting products, services, or brands using digital channels. Digital marketing is effective for several reasons:

- **Global reach:** Enables businesses to reach a global audience regardless of where they are, enabling them to expand their potential customer base beyond the local limits.

- **Targeted advertising:** Digital platforms offer sophisticated targeting options, enabling businesses to target customers based on things like demographics, interests, behaviors, and preferences.

- **Cost-effectiveness:** Compared to traditional media like TV and billboards, digital marketing offers better value for your money, because you can allocate budgets and it's also often less expensive to produce.

- **Measurable results:** Digital marketing provides detailed analytics and tracking tools, enabling businesses to measure effectiveness in real time and optimize strategies for better outcomes based on performance.

- **Personalization:** Businesses can create personalized experiences through targeted messaging and tailored content.

- **Interactivity:** Digital channels like social media, interactive websites, and email allow for two-way communication.

- **Flexibility:** Digital campaigns can be changed in real time, enabling businesses to be agile and maximize efficiencies based on market factors.

- **Brand authority:** By consistently delivering valuable content to their audience across digital channels, businesses can enhance their visibility, foster relationships, and build trust.

With digital marketing, it's almost as if businesses can have one-on-one experiences with their customers. This is really important. Digital marketing enables businesses to deliver relevant content to customers and share information about products that consumers actually want to know about. It also fosters stronger relationships and develops stronger customer loyalty. When a business understands a customer intimately—their behaviors and specific preferences—they can deliver the option to buy straight to their phone. Digital channels that offer interactivity provide great opportunities for engagement, feedback, and sharing. All these things are what make digital marketing exceptional.

VISUAL REPRESENTATION

7 ELEMENTS OF DIGITAL MARKETING—AND PRIMARY PURPOSE	
1. Website	• Presence • Information • Visibility
2. SEO	• Attraction • Credibility
3. Content marketing	• Generation of interest • Information • Perception
4. Social media marketing	• Loyalty • Engagement • Association • Awareness
5. Email marketing	• Engagement • Loyalty • Incentive

6. PPC advertising	• Connection with target audience • Visibility
7. Measurement	• Informed decision-making • Optimization • Improvement

The Basics

Digital marketing encompasses a wide range of strategies and tactics aimed at promoting products, services, and brands using digital channels. With digital marketing, the steps in the marketing funnel happen all at once, in one place. In one interaction, brands can create awareness, generate interest, and convert a sale. It's magical, when done right. Successful digital marketing campaigns often integrate multiple components to create an ecosystem of engagement.

While the specific components of digital marketing can vary depending on the goals, target audience, and industry, there are a few fundamental elements included in most digital marketing campaigns. A good place to start is understanding the following basic components:

Website: Your Foundation for Online Presence

A well-designed and user-friendly website serves as the foundation for all digital marketing efforts, making it a good place to start. It's the primary online presence where potential customers can learn about your business.

Key elements include:

- Clear navigation
- Compelling content
- Responsive design for mobile devices
- Clear call to action

Search Engine Optimization (SEO): How to Be Found

The goal of SEO is to increase organic (nonpaid) traffic to your website. SEO involves optimizing content on your website to improve its visibility and ranking in search engine results pages. What this means is that your site is found when people are looking for information relevant to what you offer.

Essential elements include:

- Keyword search
- On-page optimization (e.g., meta tags, headers, content)
- Off-page optimization (e.g., backlink-building)
- Technical optimization (e.g., site speed, mobile-friendliness)

Content Marketing: The Information You Provide

Content marketing focuses on creating and distributing valuable, relevant, and consistent content to attract and engage a target audience. Content can take on various forms. The goal is to provide helpful information, answer questions, and address pain points to build trust and establish thought leadership.

Forms of content can include:

- Blog posts
- Articles
- Videos

- Infographics
- Podcasts
- Social media posts

AHA!

According to Sprout Social, a social media management platform, these are the types of content that marketers say are the most valuable for social goals:

- *54% video*
- *53% images*
- *30% text-based posts*
- *26% stories*
- *25% live video*

Social Media Marketing: Leveraging Online Communities

Social media platforms offer opportunities to connect with and engage with your target audience directly. Social media marketing involves sharing content on social media channels. It is used to build brand awareness, foster relationships, and drive website traffic. It also includes paid advertising options to reach specific demographics and target audiences.

Social media channels may include:

- Facebook
- X
- Instagram
- LinkedIn
- TikTok
- Snapchat

AHA!

Just to clarify, social media channels can be used organically, which means at no cost, or by paying for advertising on social media platforms to reach specific audiences.

Email Marketing: Sending Emails

Email marketing involves sending targeted messages to a list of subscribers with the goal of nurturing leads, retaining customers, and driving conversions. Effective email marketing requires segmentation, personalization, and monitoring of key metrics like open rates and click-through rates.

The following chart contains guidelines for email open rates, which are the percentage of recipients who open an email campaign compared to the total number of recipients.

Open Rate	Percentage of Emails Sent
Below average	Less than 20%
Average	20%–25%
Above average	25%–30%
High/Exceptional	40%–50%

PRO TIP

To improve average or below-average email open rates, consider revising your content or subject lines to be more meaningful or intriguing to recipients. Also, this may be a good time to clean your email contacts list or revisit your targeting strategy.

Email campaigns can include:

- Newsletters

- Promotional offers

- Product updates

- Sales announcements

- Personalized content based on user preferences and behavior

Ways to develop an email marketing list are:

- Purchase a list, which is generally not recommended due to quality and trust issues. You can go online to research email list providers.

- Build your own organic email list.

  o Put opt-in forms on your website.

  o Offer promotional offers.

  o Create a loyalty program.

We've included more about email marketing later in this chapter.

Pay-per-Click (PPC) Advertising: Online Advertising

PPC advertising enables businesses to display ads on search engines (e.g., Google Ads) and other digital platforms (e.g., social media, display networks) and pay only when users click on their ads. PPC campaigns target specific keywords, demographics, or user interests to drive traffic to websites, generate leads, or increase sales. Advertisers bid on keywords and compete for ad placement in search engine results or on other platforms.

Analytics and Data Analysis: Measuring to Optimize Effectiveness of Campaigns

Analyzing data is crucial for optimizing digital marketing campaigns and measuring their effectiveness. By tracking and analyzing data, marketers can identify areas for improvement, refine their strategies, and allocate resources more effectively.

Tools like Google Analytics provide insights into:

- Website traffic

- User behavior

- Conversion rates

- Other key metrics

What we have covered includes the basic components of digital marketing. The landscape evolves with new technologies, platforms, and trends. Keep up with the changes, and adapt accordingly.

WORKSHEET

CREATING COMPELLING EMAIL SUBJECTS

A good email marketing subject line is essential for capturing the attention of your subscribers and encouraging them to open your email. It is not enough to simply send an email to a lot of people.

LIKE ALL MARKETING, AN EMAIL CAMPAIGN MUST BE THESE THREE THINGS

1. Relevant to the recipient

2. Inspiring enough to open

3. Motivating enough to take action

Without these three things, you are simply "whistling into a well," as the saying goes.

HERE ARE SOME THINGS YOU CAN DO TO ENSURE YOUR MESSAGE IS EFFECTIVE

- ☐ **Relevant:** The subject line should be relevant to the content of the email and aligned with the interests and needs of the audience. It should clearly convey what the email is about and why it's valuable to the recipient.

- ☐ **Clear:** Keep the subject line clear and concise. Avoid using overly complicated language or obscure references that may be confusing. A straightforward subject line is likelier to be understood and clicked on.

- ☐ **Personalized:** Use the recipient's name to grab their attention to make the email feel more special to them. Use data such as past purchases or browsing history to tailor subject lines.

- ☐ **Urgency:** Creating a sense of urgency in the subject line can encourage action to avoid missing out on a time-sensitive offer or limited-time promotion. Phrases like "This Weekend Only" or "Last Chance" can create a sense of urgency.

- ☐ **Scarcity:** Limited availability can also be used to create a sense of urgency, such as "Limited-Time Offer" or "Before Tickets Sell Out."

- ☐ **Curiosity:** Engage your subscribers by using a subject line that hints at valuable information or an intriguing offer. Avoid being too vague and mysterious, and avoid giving away too much information so that they will want to open the email to find out more.

- ☐ **Benefit-oriented:** Focus on what recipients will gain or learn from opening the email by highlighting the benefits or value proposition in the subject line. For example: "Discover 5 Tips to Boost Your Productivity" or "Unlock Exclusive Savings Inside."

- ☐ **Avoid spam triggers:** Steer clear of spammy-sounding words or phrases that could trigger spam filters and cause your emails to land in spam folders. Examples include excessive use of exclamation points, all caps, or words like "free" or "urgent" in all caps.

- ☐ **Avoid sounding salesy:** Being too salesy, aggressive, or pushy feels off-putting and inauthentic. Be careful about how you craft your message. There is a fine line between urgency and aggressiveness.

- ☐ **A/B testing:** Test different subject lines to see which ones perform best with your audience. Use A/B testing to experiment with different language, tones, keywords, and offers to find out which subject lines garner the most attention.

Remember that just because you have sent something in an email doesn't mean it's effective. Collect data, and build lists of people interested in receiving communication from your business.

Email Database

Let's talk about ways in which you can create an email database of your most important customers.

One way is to buy a list; however, there are ethical and legal considerations when it comes to email marketing. Purchasing an email list is generally discouraged and may even violate antispam laws such as the CAN-SPAM Act in the United States and the GDPR (General Data Protection Regulation) in the European Union.[3] Purchased lists are often discouraged because they can have low-quality data (outdated or inaccurate email addresses), can create spam complaints by sending unsolicited emails, and can be seen as simply unethical. All of this has the potential to annoy people receiving your email and damage your reputation.

A better way to build a list is by building your own opt-in email list organically by providing opportunities for people to voluntarily subscribe to your email list. Here are some ways you can do this:

- **Website sign-up forms:** Offer incentives such as discounts, free resources, or exclusive content to encourage sign-ups.

- **Content upgrades:** Offer things like e-books, white papers, or guides in exchange for email addresses. These can be promoted on your website or social media channels.

- **Events and webinars:** Host events or webinars, and collect addresses from people who register to attend. Follow up after the event to provide information and nurture the relationship.

- **Social media:** Use social media to promote your email list, and provide incentives to sign up.

- **Referral programs:** Implement a referral program where existing subscribers can refer friends in exchange for rewards and other incentives.

---

3   For more details on the CAN-Spam Act, see https://www.fcc.gov/general/can-spam#:~:text=Congress%20passed%20the%20CAN%2DSPAM,phones—not%20email%20in%20general. For more information on GDPR see https://gdpr.eu.

- **Networking:** Use in-person networking to meet new people, and add them to your list. Be sure to only include those who express a genuine interest in receiving communications from your business and provide their consent to be added to the list.

AHA!

Marketing and digital marketing require creating and distributing valuable, relevant, and consistent content.

Digital Display Advertising Made Easy

Digital marketing is a broad term that encompasses a wide range of activities. We went deeper into email marketing, and we'd like to go further into digital advertising so you are aware of the options available to you:

- **Banner ads:** These are ads that appear on websites and come in various sizes. They can be static (still) or animated.

- **Interstitial ads:** These are full-screen ads that appear between content pages or during transitions. They are often used in mobile apps.

- **Rich-media ads:** These ads incorporate interactive elements such as video or animation. They can expand when clicked.

- **Video ads:** These ads play before, during, or after online video content. They're usually short, about six seconds, and can be skippable or not skippable.

- **Native ads:** These are ads that blend into the content, matching the style and format of the platform they appear on. They seem more natural and less intrusive.

- **Social media ads:** These are ads that are formatted to social media platforms and their specific user experiences.

- **Remarketing ads:** These ads target users who have previously visited a website or interacted with a brand but may not have made a purchase.

- **Programmatic ads:** These ads are bought and sold through real-time bidding platforms using data to target specific audiences.

- **Email ads:** These ads can be included in emails sent to subscribers.

We understand that digital marketing can seem complicated. Break down complex concepts into simple, actionable steps.

....

In Summary

By using digital marketing, brands can insert themselves in almost every aspect of a consumer's daily life, on their terms, alongside content they find relevant.

- ✓ *Digital marketing can be cheap and effective.*

- ✓ *That doesn't mean it's easy; pay careful attention to creating the right messages for the right audience.*

- ✓ *Optimize your digital marketing efforts by tracking and analyzing their success.*

- ✓ *Include the right people on the lists, use relevant channels, and create applicable content.*

....

7

ADVERTISING AND PROMOTIONS

Advertising and promotions drive customer engagement, boost sales, and enhance brands. Like many of the topics we've addressed, advertising and promotions can become complicated. That's why we like advertising and promotions that work simply, and simply work. Today's consumers are bombarded with information and don't want to work hard to cut through the clutter; make things as simple as possible.

Promotions are often used to incentivize or incite purchases. They are specifically designed to attract customers and increase sales. Some examples of the types of promotions you can consider follow. As with most things in marketing, it's important that your promotions have these three things:

1. Measurable objectives

2. Alignment with your brand purpose and promise

3. Elements that can be leveraged beyond the sales transaction

PRO TIP

A forgiving return policy is a great way to lower the barrier to purchase and instill consumer confidence in your product or service. Think of the mattress company that gives you "100 sleeps," because you need a decent trial period or a cosmetics store that will take back a used product, because you need time to see if it works for your skin.

Types of Promotions

There are several basic types of promotions. You can find the type of promotion that works best for what you're selling and what's most aligned with your brand and your customer. Once you decide on the type of promotion you want to use, you can customize it for what you want to achieve and tailor it to those people you want to reach.

Here are some types of promotions you can use to drive sales and enhance brand awareness:

- **Discounts and coupons:** This is one of the most traditional and effective promotional tactics. This can include percentage discounts, BOGO (buy one, get one), BOGOHO (buy one, get one half off), or dollar-off coupons.
    - *Best for:* products
    - *The pros:* They are easy and do a good job of motivating customers to buy.
    - *The cons:* They don't necessarily drive loyalty and may erode your brand value. It is also difficult to limit exposure, not knowing how many people may claim the offer.

WARNING

Discounts can work against you if you don't pay careful attention. At one time, A&W released a one-third-pound burger to rival McDonald's Quarter Pounder. It failed despite the fact it was a bigger burger for the same price. The problem was that consumers thought one-fourth was bigger than one-third because four is bigger than three.

- **Contests and sweepstakes:** They are used to encourage engagement and participation. They often involve asking customers to perform certain actions, such as sharing personal information for entry (sharing content, submitting photos, answering questions, signing up, or making a purchase) for a chance to win prizes.

    o *Best for:* any business willing to commit to this type of promotion

    o *The pros:* They can be easy and do a good job of motivating customers to buy. They have winners you can announce. They can be tailored to have lots of brand relevance.

    o *The cons:* They require some level of participation, and not everyone wins. They also require rules and legalities that many businesses aren't necessarily prepared to deal with or have the time to implement.

- **Loyalty programs:** These programs reward customers for repeat purchases or other forms of engagement. This can include earning points for every purchase, receiving exclusive discounts or rewards, or gaining access to VIP events.

    o *Best for:* services or niche businesses

    o *The pros:* They provide a platform for engaging your most important customers.

      ○ *The cons:* They can become cumbersome for people to join and more trouble than they're worth to manage.

AHA!

Celebrations can be very effective in bringing in your best customers for a birthday or anniversary giveaway. They're also a great excuse for collecting this level of consumer data.

- **Product bundling:** This involves selling multiple products or services together as a package or at a discounted price. This encourages customers to purchase more items while also delivering value.

      ○ *Best for:* products, bundling products, or adding services to products (e.g., warranties, insurance)

      ○ *The pros:* These are attractive to consumers and offer great opportunities for companies to do upselling and cross-selling.

      ○ *The cons:* They may not necessarily encourage loyalty if the deal is all the customer is after.

- **Free samples or trials:** Offering free samples or trials enables customers to experience a product or service before making a purchase. It can help generate interest and drive future sales.

      ○ *Best for:* new products and subscriptions

      ○ *The pros:* It is a great way to introduce a new customer.

      ○ *The cons:* They can cost a lot for product and distribution.

- **Flash sales:** Also known as limited-time offers or clearance sales. These types of sales create a sense of urgency by offering steep discounts for a short period of time. Businesses can quickly drive sales and clear out extra inventory.
    - *Best for:* mature products or products reaching the end of their shelf life
    - *The pros:* It is a great way to introduce a new or value-conscious customer.
    - *The cons:* They may not create loyalists or have a residual effect on consumers.

- **Referral programs:** Referral programs incentivize existing customers to refer friends, family, or colleagues to the business. This can be done through discounts, credits, or other rewards for both the referred customer and the person who is doing the referring.
    - *Best for:* considered purchases or high-ticket items
    - *The pros:* People trust people they know.
    - *The cons:* This depends on the willingness of your customers to offer a referral, and too many referrals can be overwhelming.

- **Seasonal promotions:** These types of promotions tie into holidays, events, or specific times of the year. Using seasonal promotions, businesses can leverage timing around other events to create themed promotions, special offers, or limited-edition products to capitalize on seasonal trends.
    - *Best for:* seasonal products and services
    - *The pros:* You have the opportunity to ride the wave of another influential element to boost sales.
    - *The cons:* You don't want to rely on other events to drive sales, so you'll want to consider how to maintain a lasting impression.

These are a few ways to structure your promotions. Businesses often combine multiple tactics to create integrated and effective promotional campaigns. Ultimately, the choice of promotion type depends on three things:

1. Target audience
2. Marketing objectives
3. Budget considerations

WARNING

Don't get carried away with promotions. Too many promotions can devalue the brand and have the potential to confuse customers. Make your marketing smart, consistent, and focused for greater impact— including your promotions.

Evaluation

It is important to provide a recap of your promotion after it is completed and the promotional period is over in order to measure the response and value. Evaluations help assess whether or not the program was successful and provide an opportunity to reflect and to decide if you want to do it again. Many times, you may want to have the promotion again but with some changes and adjustments. This process helps you evaluate, measure, and refine. Or it can help you decide if it's worth repeating. A thoughtful evaluation process helps ensure you're investing your marketing dollars wisely.

We've included a worksheet on the following page that you can use to evaluate your promotions.

WORSHEET

PROMOTION EVALUATION

....

Title: the name or theme of the promotion

Goal: the purpose of the promotion

Specifics: who, what, where, when, and how?

What worked?

What didn't work?

How can it be improved?

What can be done differently next time? Will there be a next time?

Are there other risks or practical considerations to include?

What is the recommendation for this promotion moving forward?

Leveraging Promotions

When developing ideas for promotions, it's important to think about what you can do to leverage the promotion, by getting more out of it than just the direct sales benefit of the promotion itself. Some ways you can leverage promotions follow:

- **Has a public relations component:** This is an element you can use to get earned media, like announcing a winner.

- **Is ownable:** This is something that is unique and ownable to your company or product.

- **Can be repeatable:** This is something that can become an annual event that people can come to expect from you.

- **Provides an opportunity for collecting data:** If your promotion involves collecting consumer data, make sure you consider ways to utilize the data for customer engagement.

When it comes to incentives, there are two especially important rules:

1. **Make it an added value:** By adding something, or "sweetening the deal," this avoids discounting the brand value.

2. **Make it timely:** Putting a distinct time frame around a promotion creates a sense of urgency for consumers to "act now."

Cause-Related Marketing

Cause-related marketing involves partnering with a charitable organization or supporting a social cause as part of a promotional campaign. This not only benefits the cause but also enhances the brand's reputation and attracts socially conscious customers. Research suggests that consumers express a preference for companies that have a point of view and stand for something with purpose. Being a socially responsible company is an effective way to develop a deeper level of engagement among consumers. This approach creates alignment between what customers value and the values that brands represent. Customers don't just buy products and services; they buy trust, and trust comes from having shared values.

Consumer trends indicate that today's consumer values fall within these four primary categories:

1. **Kindness:** As consumers look to demonstrations of kindness to counterbalance negativity, they seek consistent and routine demonstrations of kindness.

2. **Authenticity:** As Big Data grows, humanizing technology and transactions becomes increasingly important. Consumers seek more authentic and meaningful experiences, sense of place, and brand interaction.

3. **Community:** In a digitally connected, digitally social, and digitally sharing world, consumers focus on building "community."

4. **Purpose:** Consumers define who they are by what they identify with and seek brands with values that align with their own values.

The solution to making a brand connection with consumer values is to develop a cause-marketing strategy. This is where a company aligns its brand with a social or environmental cause to mutually benefit both the business and the cause. It involves promoting the cause through marketing campaigns, often by donating a portion of sales or raising awareness, with the goal of enhancing brand reputation, customer loyalty, and driving sales while also supporting a worthy cause. Supporting local communities or specific causes is not just an important business tool; it's an important marketing tool. It offers personal relevance by providing a link between social and business values. It means a lot to consumers to know that they are supporting businesses that do good things. Also, people want to know about the good things that businesses are doing.

Association with good causes encourages engagement by connecting a favorable aspect with the brand. It incites positive change by bringing people together. To implement corporate social responsibility, businesses can effectively take cause marketing from a business plan to a marketing plan in three steps:

1. **Strategy:** Develop a strategy. Determine how the giving focus links to the company's purpose, products, and industry. For example, national banks may connect with local communities by supporting local causes that are meaningful to residents and community members. This makes them feel localized and connected to customers.

2. **Execute/Implement:** Leverage cause-marketing efforts to maximize impact. Determine how you can leverage the strategy to foster customer and employee belief in the company. For example, your business can create opportunities for employees to participate so that they feel more connected to the cause.

3. **Optimize:** Engage partnerships, sponsorships, and strategic alliances. Determine the best partners to achieve your mission and deliver your message. For example, find out what your partners can do to deliver your message of support for their cause.

Corporate Social Responsibility (CSR) is largely about bold leadership and vision. It shows an organization's commitment to its people and customers. Ultimately, the long-term effects of CSR pay real dividends.

Influencer Collaborations

An influencer is someone who has the power to affect the purchasing decisions of others because of their authority, knowledge, position, or relationship with their audience. They typically have a large and engaged following on social media platforms, blogs, podcasts, or other online or broadcast channels. Influencers are often considered experts in their field or trendsetters in specific niches, such as food, fashion, travel, sports, fitness, music, and beauty.

Partnering with influencers or celebrities to promote products or services can help businesses reach new audiences and build credibility. Influencers create content featuring the brand and share it with their followers, often in exchange for compensation, free trips, or free products.

Regarding social media promotions, targeting customers online through your social media channels can be easy and cost-effective. This is an effective way for businesses to engage with their audience, encourage sharing, increase brand visibility, and drive conversions.

Social Media Promotions

Here are some ways you can consider using social media for promotions:

- **Contests and giveaways:** Ask followers to like, share, or comment on a post for a chance to win a prize. Prizes could be a product, service, gift card, a combination of things, or an exclusive experience.

  Example: An ice cream shop might run a giveaway where followers have to tag friends and follow the store's page to win a free scoop of ice cream.

- **Flash sales and limited-time offers:** Create urgency by promoting exclusive discounts or deals that are available for a limited-time only.

  Example: A boutique clothing store might offer 24-hour flash-sale discounts to its social media followers.

- **User-generated content (UGC) campaigns:** Encourage customers to share photos, videos, and reviews of your products or services. Reposting UGC not only showcases customer satisfaction, but also encourages others to engage with your brand.

  Example: A travel agency might ask customers to share their vacation photos using a branded hashtag.

AHA!

User-generated content holds more value: It always means more when someone endorses you than trying to convince customers of something yourself.

- **Polls and surveys:** Using social media polls or surveys to gather feedback from your audience is an excellent way to generate engagement and learn more about your customers' preferences. Ask followers to vote on their favorite product feature or provide input on potential new products, product extensions, or product features.

  Example: A local restaurant could run a contest to encourage followers to participate by submitting their own content, such as making a recommendation for a favorite drink or appetizer to be featured as the monthly special.

- **Exclusive offers:** Reward your followers with exclusive discounts that are only available to them. Not only can this help foster good will among your customers, but it can leverage a sense of loyalty and incentivize more people to engage with your brand on social media.

  Example: A photographer could offer a special package for customers around the holiday season to promote gift-giving, or an art gallery could offer a special VIP-only reception an hour before an event. There's a lot you could leverage by offering something special to client VIPs to encourage them to share their experience.

- **Collaborations:** Partner with influencers or content creators in your industry to promote your products or services to their followers. You can give them free products or free access (if it's a venue) or other monetary compensation in exchange for positive promotion of your brand through their social media channels to reach their network. Influencer networks are usually very large and include trusted fans who are interested in similar things. Influencers can create sponsored posts, reviews, or tutorials featuring your brand or service, thereby reaching a wider audience and building credibility.

Example: Invite an influencer to a VIP tour of your facility. Give them behind-the-scenes access for added-value interest so they can create never-before-seen footage, adding entertainment components to their audience while touting the attributes of your business and its products or services.

- **Live Q&A sessions:** This could also take the form of a webinar if there's a more instructional or informative side to what your business offers. Host live question-and-answer sessions on social media platforms to interact with your audience in real time. During these sessions, you can provide valuable insights or tips while showcasing your expertise in your field. This is an excellent way to demonstrate thought leadership through delivering expert advice.

  Example: A real estate agent may give advice on topics for selling and buying a home, such as how to stage a home for selling or what features sell.

Hashtag campaigns: Create branded hashtags, and encourage followers to use them when posting content related to your brand or a specific campaign. This can help increase visibility and engagement on social media platforms.

Example: On Fridays, a fitness brand might create a hashtag like #FitnessFriday and encourage followers to share their workout routines.

AHA!

A hashtag is a word or phrase preceded by the "#" symbol and is used on social media platforms to categorize content and make it easily searchable. It helps users find posts or topics related to a specific theme or subject by clicking on or searching for that hashtag.

- **Interactive content:** Try experimenting with interactive formats such as quizzes, polls, or interactive stories to engage your audience and encourage participation. This type of content can be fun and engaging while also generating higher levels of interaction and sharing.

  Example: A flower shop might ask customers what their favorite flower is and why and then create a "flower personality" using customer content to tell the story.

> **PRO TIP**
> *When it comes to social media promotions, the key is to be creative, authentic, and provide value to your audience while staying true to your brand and aligning with your overall marketing objectives.*

Promotions

Sales promotions are great tools to drive customer engagement, boost sales, and enhance your brand. There are a few rules that apply to almost all types of promotions; they are:

- Consider adding value rather than offering a discount.
- Have a clear call to action.
- Keep it simple.
- Create a sense of urgency.

> **PRO TIP**
> *When it comes to promotions, simple is better. Consumers have busy lives and limited time and attention.*

There are many types of promotions that businesses can employ. Let's review some common types of promotions and their benefits:

- **Discounts:** These can come in the form of reduced price by percentage, dollar-amount-off regular price, or bundle discounts that encourage customers to buy multiple items at a reduced price for the bundle.

- **Coupons:** These are printed and distributed through direct mail or digital coupons distributed online.

- **Flash sales:** These are short-term sales events, often with a limited quantity or time frame, creating a sense of urgency.

- **Loyalty programs:** Reward customers for repeat purchases by offering discounts, free products, merchandise, or exclusive access.

- **Contests and sweepstakes:** Encourage engagement by giving customers a chance to win prizes through participation.

- **Free samples:** Give free product samples to customers to encourage trial and purchase.

- **Cash-back offers:** Give customers a percentage of their purchase back as cash or a discount on a future purchase.

- **BOGO (buy one, get one) and BOGOHO (buy one, get one half off):** Offer a free or discounted item with a qualifying purchase.

- **LTOs (limited-time offers):** Create a sense of urgency and exclusivity by promoting limited-time deals.

- **Referral programs:** Encourage customers to refer friends and family in exchange for discounts or cash bonuses.

- **Seasonal promotions:** Tailor promotions to specific holidays, seasons, or events.

- **Cross-selling and upselling:** Encourage customers to buy related or upgraded products.

- **Guarantees or warranties:** Offer extended warranties or satisfaction guarantees to instill confidence and encourage purchases.

- **Trade-in offers:** Offer discounts or credits for trading in old products when purchasing new ones.

- **Cause-related marketing:** Tie promotions to charitable causes demonstrating corporate social responsibility and making consumers feel better about their purchase choice.

- **Membership programs:** Offer exclusive deals, early access, or special perks to members.

- **Limited editions or exclusive releases:** Create scarcity and demand by offering unique or exclusive products.

- **Partnerships and collaborations:** Join other brands to create joint promotions, special events, or unique offers.

- **Customer appreciation sales:** Show gratitude to existing customers with special discounts or promotions.

- **Email and social media promotions:** Use email or social media platforms to share exclusive offers.

When designing a sales and marketing promotion, it's crucial to align the promotion with your overall marketing strategy (including customer acquisition strategy, as applicable), target audience, and business objectives. As with all marketing tactics, testing and measuring the effectiveness of different promotions can help refine future approaches to promotions.

WARNING

Unless you want to be in the business of discounting, avoid discounts; consider added-value incentives instead. This approach helps keep your brand value intact.

WARNING

When it comes to designing promotions, have an understanding of the potential financial exposure. For example, you may want to limit the offer to the first 100 people so that you have limited cost exposure (as opposed to unlimited offer redemption).

In Summary

✓ *Promotions are beneficial occasionally but should not be a given.*

✓ *When it comes to promotions, simple is better and so is urgency. Create a short, specific time frame for participation.*

✓ *Add value instead of discounting.*

✓ *Corporate social responsibility can become a key aspect of your marketing strategy if it is focused, authentic, and ownable.*

8

CREATIVE

In advertising and in marketing, the term "creative" is typically used to refer to the imaginative and innovative aspects of developing campaigns, advertising, or content used to communicate a message to consumers about a product or service offering. It encompasses the process of generating original ideas, concepts, and designs to effectively communicate a message, identify a business offering, or promote something. It can involve many aspects of the messaging, such as copywriting, visual identity, design, storytelling, and multimedia production, all aimed at capturing the attention of the audience and inspiring action.

Marketing includes developing creative assets to fuel your marketing efforts by formulating your message and delivering it to the right people in the most effective way possible. The process of developing the stuff that's used in marketing and advertising is often referred to simply as "creative" because it's more than the assets. It's how you creatively solve problems.

Developing creative solutions is not creative simply for the sake of being creative. It has a direction and a purpose so that the messaging is attention-getting. Most of all, it serves its purpose by delivering a message.

Creativity is the driving force behind compelling marketing efforts. It sparks innovation, captures attention, and leaves a lasting impression. Creative assets, when done right, can tell a compelling story that resonates with the people who matter most: the people who buy your products and services.

> **PRO TIP**
>
> *Creative assets are what's used to tell a brand story. Consider what you'll need from the beginning. Make a list of all of the creative applications you'll want as a final deliverable—this way you can make asset development part of the campaign strategy and not miss including anything in the process.*

Simply stated, creative assets are the things that are used in marketing campaigns, such as images, ads, videos, and signs. Assets can be broken down further by type:

- **Identity:** logos, colors, design elements, and product images
- **Digital assets:** videos, still images, banner ads, and social media posts
- **Print assets:** posters, billboards, and flyers
- **Trade show:** name badges, trade-show booth panels, and promotional giveaways
- **Retail:** point-of-sale materials, promotional signage, and displays

Having a variety of creative assets should support your marketing strategies. Brands create a unique identity through the quality and consistency of their creative. Brands create a "look" that's made up of many creative elements, including tone, style, color, and presentation. For example, when you see something from Dove, you know it's from Dove. This brand consistently delivers on a look, feel, and message that is consistent with its promise of "real beauty."

When creative assets are consistent, they work harder. When a customer can easily identify a piece of communication with your business, it makes it that much more effective in obtaining the attention of the target audience and getting your message across.

Creative assets work together to tell a story. A customer will see a billboard that may instill a level of awareness about your brand. Then they see a commercial that provides them with more context for what your product or service offers. Then they are hit with a digital ad online that takes them directly to an e-commerce site where they can browse specific product options and convert to a sale. Each asset in the journey tells a different part of the story and serves a different purpose. When they work together, that helps consumers in making purchase decisions.

Where Does Creative Come From?

Everyone is creative to some extent. Online design tools make creating creative assets easier than ever. However, creative design and messaging in marketing are a trained skill set. Typically, creative assets entail a visual and audio (or written) component. The copy, paired with an image, creates an idea and a message designed to tell a story of a brand in a way that resonates with the audience. When done well, the consumer will think that brand understands them and the product they need.

As a business owner, business operator, or entrepreneur, you have options when it comes to creative resources. You can use a full-service agency that has resources to manage everything from creating your marketing strategy to developing the assets to planning and buying the media to tracking results and optimizing your efforts. Or you can find a "freelancer," a creative expert who works independently and has access to other specialists like copywriters and producers. There are many options in between.

Before seeking a resource, know your needs and budget.

Guidelines for Providing Creative Direction

- **Deliverable:** What is the final product or desired outcome? (Example: a printed 5X7-inch mailer or a digital ad.)

- **Deadline:** When does this need to be completed? (Example: a printable PDF uploaded by noon on September 5.)

- **Target audience:** Who is this directed to? (Example: moms who have young children, whose pain points are time and money, and who are motivated by quality and convenience.)

- **Purpose:** What is the purpose of this effort? (Example: to get moms to adopt this product as their product of choice because it's healthy for their kids, and if it's good for their kids, then it implies they must be good parents.)

- **Information:** What are the supporting points of the effort? (Example: the benefits of the product.)

- **Call to action:** What do you want the intended audience to do? (Example: online or in-store purchases.)

- **Mandatories:** What are the elements that must be included? (Example: logos or disclaimers.)

- **Existing assets:** Provide any existing assets. (Example: images or logos.)

  Examples: Provide examples of things you like or find inspiring. Share examples of communications from the competition.

PRO TIP

Creative execution of an idea is what sets a brand apart from the competition and drives real business results. It's the quality of the idea that matters most; almost anyone can execute.

Guidelines for Providing Creative Feedback

We wanted to provide general guidelines for how to deliver constructive feedback for maximum effectiveness. When you give great input and better feedback, you get better results. It's really important to know how to give feedback in order to get what you need in order to accomplish what you set out to accomplish.

Following these guidelines will alleviate headaches, reduce revisions, and enhance the relationship with your creative or design team:

- **Find the problems, not the solutions.** Explain what you think isn't working, and allow them to solve it.

- **Share your opinions, but don't tell them what to do.** Trust that this is their area of expertise and that they work best when they can maintain a sense of ownership.

- **Stay focused on the goal.** Revisit the original brief or direction, and focus on the project's target audience and goals.

- **Ask questions.** This creates dialogue and encourages collaboration that leads to a stronger final product. Posing questions will give you better insight, and you might discover their version solves potential issues you hadn't considered.

- **Consolidate your feedback.** Designate a point person in your organization to consolidate feedback and/or consider limiting the number of people giving feedback.

- **Don't forget to explain what you like.** Discussing successful elements is just as valuable as going over areas that need more polishing. This will keep your relationship healthy and morale high.

- **Comment with the audience in mind.** Remember that *you* are not necessarily the target audience.

- **Be specific.** If it's not legible, say so instead of using vague comments like "Make it pop" or "Jazz it up." Look for examples that demonstrate what you're looking for and then explain what you like about them.

- **Be direct and honest.** But pay attention to tone and wording. Saying that you found something confusing is more productive than saying, "No one will understand this."

PRO TIP
Your marketing message needs to be clear and easy to read and legibly convey one thing.

Good Creative

Creative is subjective. However, good creative in advertising typically adheres to several key criteria. Just as it's important to provide feedback in a constructive way, it's a good idea to judge and evaluate based on the factors that make creative messaging in advertising effective. Let's look at the key criteria when it comes to good creative in advertising.

- **Relevant:** The creative concept should be relevant to the brand, product, or service being advertised. It must also be relevant to the target audience. This is why financial institutions have advertising that's different from that of sushi restaurants. They are vastly different products, in different categories, serving different consumer needs.

- **Original:** The advertising should be fresh, unique, and distinctive, standing out from competitors and capturing the attention of the intended audience. "Different" doesn't mean "weird for the sake of being different" but rather "being intentional in approach and not trying to be like all the others."

- **Honest:** Advertising needs to be truthful. Brand trust may be the ultimate consumer currency.

- **Memorable:** The creative should be memorable, leaving a lasting impression on the audience, and making the brand or message stick in their minds.

- **Clear:** The message should be easy to understand. You are competing with a lot of information and noise in the marketplace. Clarity is the best way to avoid confusion or ambiguity. Trying to be too clever or tell an inside story doesn't usually work in advertising.

  Clarity in messaging means: having content that's easy to read and understand.

  Determine your messaging hierarchy up front. Rank your most important points in order of importance. Here are three examples:

  1. *Buy one, get one free:* prioritizing the offer
  2. *Limited-time offer, Presidents' Day Sale:* creating a sense of urgency
  3. *Available only online—link here:* providing a clear and easy call to action

- **Call to action:** Your advertising should prompt people to take action and tell them what you want them to do (whether it's making a purchase, going to a store, visiting a website, or engaging with the brand in some other way). Have a clear call to action on every piece of content and communication with customers.

- **Emotional resonance:** Effective advertising often evokes emotions—whether it's humor, empathy, excitement, or nostalgia—connecting with consumers on a deeper level.

- **Engagement:** The creative and the message should engage with the audience, encouraging interaction, sharing, or wanting to learn more about the brand or product.

- **Adaptable:** Good creative posts should be adaptable to various media formats and platforms, ensuring the creative remains effective across print, digital, social media, and other channels. Before you land on a direction, ensure it works across various channels and executions; can be simple (e.g., an outdoor billboard); and can be used across print, video, and audio applications.

- **Measured:** Make it measurable. Ideally, the effectiveness of the creative should be measurable through metrics such as brand awareness, recall, engagement, and, ultimately, in sales and conversions. Remember—you're not just doing things to do things. Make sure your creative elements are getting the response you set out to achieve. That's how you know it's working.

....

THE A/B TESTING METHOD

Ever heard of A/B testing? This is a method used in marketing to compare two versions of a webpage, email, advertisement, or other marketing asset to determine which one performs better. You can use this method to test variables in your offer or your marketing. Here's how it works:

- ☐ **Create variations:** *Start by creating two versions of the marketing asset that you want to test. These versions should differ in one specific aspect, such as the offer, headline, imagery, or call to action.*

- ☐ **Randomized assignment:** *Visitors or recipients are randomly assigned to one of the two versions, with each group only seeing one variation. This ensures that the results are not skewed by factors such as demographics or behavior.*

- ☐ **Measure performance:** *Track relevant metrics, such as click-through rate, conversion rate, bounce rate, or revenue generated for each variation during the testing period.*

- ☐ **Statistical analysis:** *Use statistical methods to analyze the data and determine if there is a significant difference between the two variations. This typically involves calculating confidence intervals, p-values, or performing hypothesis tests.*

☐ **Choose a winner:** *Based on the results of the A/B test, identify the image or ad that performs best in achieving the marketing objectives. Move forward with confidence knowing that the winning version is likelier to perform and may be implemented for the broader audience.*

☐ **Repeat and optimize:** *Use the insights gained from the A/B test to inform future decisions. Continue to test and refine different elements to improve performance over time.*

A/B testing enables marketers to make data-driven decisions (as opposed to your best guess!) and optimize marketing efforts for better results. It helps identify which variations resonate most with your audience, leading to improved engagement, conversion rates, and overall effectiveness of marketing campaigns and specific tactics.

••

- **Consistent:** We saved this one for last because it's the single most important factor in branding and marketing. Your advertising, messaging, and visuals should maintain consistency with the brand's overall identity, tone, values, and messaging across different channels, media, and touchpoints. We cannot stress enough how important it is to be consistent.

PRO TIP

Consistency is so important to branding, advertising, and marketing that it consistently comes up.

Color and Psychology

The subject of color is interesting and meaningful when it comes to branding, product marketing, and advertising. Different colors evoke various emotions and perceptions in consumers. For example, red can convey excitement or urgency, while blue may represent trust and reliability. Advertisers strategically use color to represent their product or brand and to influence perceptions by creating associations and desired responses. Understanding the psychological impact of colors can help advertisers effectively communicate their messages and connect with their audiences on a deeper level.

Although the color spectrum is broad, here's a fun exploration of what different basic colors may convey in advertising. Remember, you are not the audience and, while your personal preferences may play a role, you must consider how elements like color play into the consumer psyche and decision-making process.

- **Red:** The color red conveys excitement, energy, urgency, and passion and can stimulate appetite. It is often used to grab attention and create a sense of agency or excitement. As an example, think of McDonald's, Doritos, and Coca-Cola. Red can also mean welcoming, like the Talbots red door.

- **Blue:** The color blue represents trust, reliability, professionalism, and calmness. As an example, blue is frequently used by banks, tech companies, and health-care providers to convey security and dependability. Think of Venmo, Zoom, and Bank of America.

- **Yellow:** The color yellow symbolizes optimism, warmth, and youthfulness. It's often used to grab attention and convey a sense of happiness or friendliness. Consider brands like Hertz, Denny's, Lay's potato chips, and Shell gas stations that lean into yellow.

- **Green:** An obvious color choice for its association with nature, growth, health, and wealth. Green is used to convey eco-friendliness, freshness, and relaxation. It's also commonly used in food and financial contexts. Some examples of brands that use green in their marketing are Starbucks, Whole Foods, Spotify, and Hulu.

- **Orange:** The color orange evokes feelings of excitement, enthusiasm, and creativity. It creates a sense of fun and energy, particularly in industries like entertainment and food products. Leaning into orange are brands like The Home Depot, Reese's, Nickelodeon, and Dunkin'.

- **Purple:** The color purple represents luxury, royalty, and creativity. It's used to convey a sense of sophistication and elegance, often in beauty or high-end product advertising. Purple-loving brands include Cadbury and Hallmark.

- **Pink:** The color pink symbolizes femininity, romance, and sweetness. Pink is commonly used in products targeting women or to convey a sense of care and nurturing. You can't forget pink brands such as Lyft, T-Mobile, and Victoria's Secret.

- **Black:** The color black conveys sophistication, power, and elegance. Black is often used in luxury brands to evoke a sense of exclusivity and prestige. When it comes to black, think of Uber, Adidas, and Prada.

AHA!

No matter what color you choose, all logos should be able to live in a black-and-white version. It's an unbreakable rule of identity.

- **White:** The color white represents purity, simplicity, and cleanliness. It is often used to create a minimalist, clean, or modern aesthetic, often in technology or health-care advertising. Some famous brand examples that make use of white are Apple and Nike.

- **Brown:** Associated with stability, reliability, and earthiness, brown is commonly used in advertising for natural or organic products. One of the most famous brands to use brown is UPS, so much so that, at one time, it adopted brown as its distinguishable selling point in its campaign "What can brown do for you?" UPS has used brown as its primary color since the early 20th century. Other examples of companies that have adopted brown are Hershey's and Louis Vuitton.

Color associations can vary, depending on cultural context and personal experiences, but advertisers can often leverage general perceptions to evoke specific emotions and create connections using other design elements, voice, tone, and imagery. It all works together.

AHA!
If you want to stand out in a category, consider what competitors are doing, and do something different. Uber is black, so Lyft went with pink. UPS is brown, FedEx is purple and orange, and DHL is yellow and red, giving three brands in one category color differentiation.

Let's Talk about Fonts

"Font" is a fancy term for the specific style of text that's printed on a page or displayed on a computer screen. It's the style of the letters that form words. Examples of commonly used fonts are Arial, Times New Roman, Helvetica, and Comic Sans. They can also be customized. Custom fonts are often used in logo design. Fonts play a crucial role in influencing a brand, as they can affect personality and how it's perceived. They can be a differentiator for your brand.

Here's an at-a-glance chart that addresses styles of fonts and their association.

Font	Association
Serif	Tradition, sophistication, and reliability
Sans-serif	Modern, clean, and approachable
Script	Elegance and creativity
BOLD GEOMETRIC	Strength and innovation

One of the most important aspects of fonts is legibility. Ensure that the font style and size used make the communication readable.

Signage

When it comes to signage, the key elements of good creative still apply. However, we want to call out a few things that are particularly important when it comes to signage. Signage plays a different role, whether it means identification of a place or used as a means to draw people into a retail location. Here are a few things to consider that are specific to great signage:

- **Visibility:** Signage should stand out from its surroundings and be visible from a distance. Use contrasting colors, bold fonts, and appropriate sizing to enhance visibility. If it's not visible, it won't matter what it says or how it's been designed.

PRO TIP

Test the visibility of signage in real time and space. Signs and billboards look very different on a computer screen from how they do in real life.

- **Branding:** Make sure to incorporate consistent branding elements such as logos, colors, and fonts to reinforce brand identity and recognition.

- **Location:** Place the signage in strategic locations where it will be seen by the target audience. Consider factors such as foot-traffic patterns and regulations.

- **Durability:** Use high-quality materials and printing techniques to ensure that the signage is durable and long-lasting, especially for outdoor or high-traffic environments.

Use a company specializing in signage. It can incorporate your existing marketing materials, brand guidelines, and preliminary ideas as inspiration in creating your signage program. A vendor that specializes in signage will have access to products and innovation that best works for your environment, budget, and goals.

PRO TIP

Look at printed versions of all of your communications side by side: your signage, website, digital and print ads, etc. Use this test of having everything in one place to confirm consistency of elements and clarity of primary messaging across multiple channels and applications.

....

In Summary

✓ *Good creative in advertising is always, at a minimum, clear, relevant, and consistent.*

✓ *Creative is subjective, so it's essential to have communication goals in mind and to judge creative based on its ability to achieve its goals.*

✓ *Learn how to give creative feedback for maximum effectiveness.*

✓ *Be careful not to be creative for the sake of creativity.*

✓ *Consider using A/B testing to test your creative and feel more confident about the variables that resonate with your customers.*

....

9

SPONSORSHIPS AND EVENT MARKETING

We committed a chapter to sponsorships and event marketing for a few reasons, most notably because they offer unique opportunities for brands to engage directly with their audiences, build awareness, and foster positive associations. Events provide platforms for brands to showcase products or services in relevant contexts, create engaging and memorable experiences, and establish emotional connections with consumers. They have the added benefit of being able to generate media coverage and create social media buzz, extending the reach of the brand's message and amplifying its impact.

When done right, sponsorships are a win-win in that they benefit both the event and the sponsor. The key is to find a sponsorship opportunity or event whose audience matches your customers. Pick events and brands that align with your values and complement your products or services.

> **WARNING**
> *Don't get caught in the land of logos among many other sponsors. Ensure your sponsorship dollars make sense. Have clear goals.*

What's often difficult for brands is defining the best way to use sponsorships and events to their advantage. As stated throughout, you must begin with clearly defined goals and objectives. This helps create the guardrails and plot the path for the best ways to leverage events. Many events are implemented without a strategy. They easily lend themselves to becoming a collection of logos. For this reason, we have included a form for organizing and vetting your own sponsorship opportunities so that you can use the dollars to directly benefit your brand.

WORKSHEET

HOW TO EVALUATE SPONSORSHIPS

Envision this scenario: Your business is considering sponsoring a corporate event. The event sponsorship coordinator will likely provide you with a package that outlines everything the sponsorship includes. As a sponsor, you will have the opportunity to evaluate that information to make sure it aligns with your brand's values, audiences, and value of the investment.

BUSINESS OVERVIEW:

☐ Why is this business a good fit for your business?

EVENT OVERVIEW:

☐ Who attends this event?

☐ What other businesses sponsor this event? Are you one of many or one of a select few?

☐ Why is this event an opportunity for your business?

SPONSORSHIP BENEFITS:

☐ Ability to interact with people

☐ Ability to collect data

☐ Signage opportunities

☐ Access to mailing lists

COST EVALUATION:

☐ What is the cost to sponsor the event?

☐ What value does your business provide for the event?

EXPECTATIONS:

☐ What do you expect to gain from the event?

☐ Will the event organizer work with you afterward to evaluate the event? If so, in what manner will this be accomplished?

PRACTICAL CONSIDERATIONS:

☐ Is this exclusive for your business category?

☐ What has the potential to go wrong?

☐ What is the plan to handle something that could go wrong?

☐ What are additional costs or logistics that we need to consider?

☐ What sponsorship elements are not important to you?

Sponsorships

Sponsorships are an effective way to connect with the community, create brand awareness, align with like-minded businesses, and engage with people when they're not necessarily consuming media. Sponsorships are also difficult for valuation and evaluation.

CLARITY

What's the difference between valuation and evaluation? Valuation is the process of determining the present value of an asset. Evaluation is the process of appraising the performance or effectiveness of something.

There are two common pitfalls for companies when considering sponsorships:

- **1. Engaging in sponsorships for the wrong reason:** For example, the marketing director buys the sponsorship for hockey because he likes hockey, or the CEO sponsors the golf tournament because he wants to play in it. Sometimes, this can work out if the sponsorship provides business networking opportunities, such as a suite at an NFL game where you can entertain clients. If you take this approach, be sure the tickets end up in the hands of the right people. This could mean explicit rules about the invitations (e.g., make it nontransferable).

- **2. Buying logo placements:** Logo placements as sponsorship packages are fine, but that shouldn't be all that your sponsorship entails. For most businesses, awareness alone should not be your only marketing goal. The most effective way to leverage a sponsorship is through the opportunities it offers you to engage with people.

We will talk more about how you can use sponsorships to work harder for you and your business and what you can do to measure their effectiveness.

Let's start with the factors you may want to consider when it comes to sponsorships and whether or not one makes sense for your business:

- **Brand alignment:** How well does the sponsor's brand align with yours, and do your businesses complement each other? For example, Red Bull represents energy, excitement, and adventure, which aligns well with its extreme-sports sponsorships.

- **Audience:** Do you share the same values and reach the same people? A good example of audience alignment would be Nike's partnership with the National Basketball Association that attracts millions of fans who are highly engaged with the sport and may wear Nike shoes when playing basketball themselves.

- **Reach:** What level of reach does the sponsorship offer in terms of the number of people it's exposed to and for what length of time? This could include events that are broadcast and have the potential to reach a television-viewing audience. The Super Bowl is the championship game of the National Football League, with more than 100 million viewers in the United States—for a single game.[4]

- **Engagement:** To what extent does the sponsorship enable you to directly engage with people? Example: Conduct a contest where people have to sign up to win a prize and you collect data to enhance your database.

- **Response:** The opportunity to generate interest and response from people. Coca-Cola's partnership with the FIFA World Cup, an international football (soccer) tournament organized by the Fédération Internationale de Football Association (FIFA), creates a strong consumer response. Coca-Cola releases special-edition packaging and collectible merchandise, driving consumer demand around the globe.

- **Overall impact on marketing goals:** Consider the correlation between the impact and marketing goals. This may include things like level of brand engagement, positive brand association, enhanced brand perception, and an increase in revenue. Delve into any of the examples mentioned, and you'll get a better understanding of the magnitude of impact a single smart partnership can have on driving engagement and consumer affinity for a brand.

---

4   https://www.statista.com/statistics/216526/super-bowl-us-tv-viewership/

As you consider the factors going into a sponsorship, you'll also want to measure the effectiveness of your sponsorship. Sponsorships are a little less technical when it comes to analytics. There's usually not a clear conversion rate or revenue correlation. However, there are some ways to go about analyzing the effectiveness of your sponsorships. They are:

- Return on investment: the benefits or value that a sponsor receives in return for the investment

- Reach: brand exposure

- Perception: feedback and audience sentiment

Now that we have addressed the potential pitfalls, factors to consider, and effectiveness metrics, let's look at some of the options when it comes to sponsorship assets:

- Networking event or series

- Naming rights for a venue or event

- Galas or fundraisers

- Sporting events or sports teams

- Races or series of events

- Concerts, festivals, productions, or performances

Some important things to consider when it comes to sponsorships:

- Don't get lost in the crowd.

- Evaluate and re-evaluate the sponsorship.

- Ask for data that help you understand the value.

- Consider how sponsorships complement your other marketing efforts.

Event Marketing

Event marketing has to do with what you do to actively engage with people at an event. Here are some things to consider when planning engagement at events.

To engage with consumers at events, your brand can:

- **Set clear objectives.** Define what you want to achieve from the event, whether it's increasing brand awareness, introducing new products, generating leads, or launching a new product.

- **Understand your audience.** Research and understand the demographics, interests, and preferences of the attendees to tailor your messaging and activations accordingly.

- **Create an immersive experience.** Design interactive booths, installations, or activities that engage, captivate, and encourage interaction with your brand.

- **Offer incentives.** Provide incentives such as discounts, giveaways, or exclusive access to encourage attendees to engage with your brand and provide their contact information. Use this information to build, or add to, your database.

- **Use technology.** Incorporate technology such as interactive displays, QR codes, augmented reality, or mobile apps to enhance the event experience and collect valuable information about attendees.

- **Collaborate.** Events are a great place to collaborate with influencers or other partners. Partnerships with complementary brands can extend your reach and credibility among attendees.

- **Follow up.** Capture leads, and use the information to follow up with attendees after the event with personalized emails, special offers, or invitations to continue the conversation and nurture relationships.

One of the things that's tough for people not immersed in marketing is the lingo. The marketing industry has no shortage of terminology, which adds to the complexity of it all. This book was created specifically to simplify, so that's what we'll do. Event marketing is also called "engagement marketing." Other terms you may hear related to event marketing are "experiential marketing" and "activations." Experiential marketing is a strategy that focuses on the "experiential" aspect of engagement. It focuses on creating memorable and immersive brand experiences for consumers. As for activations, this refers to what brands can do to "activate" events, which also focuses on strategies and tactics to engage people at events.

PRO TIP

Don't let marketing lingo confuse you or complicate things. Terms like "experiential marketing," "activations," and "engagement marketing" all mean basically the same thing: how brands interact with consumers at events.

In Real Life

"In real life" (also known as "IRL") in marketing refers to actions, experiences, or interactions that occur offline, outside of the digital environment. It emphasizes real-world, tangible experiences, as opposed to virtual or online interactions. Marketers have adopted the term "IRL" to emphasize the importance of physical, face-to-face interactions, such as in-person meetings, events, and product demonstrations in building relationships and driving customer engagement. This term acknowledges the significance of offline channels in the marketing mix, alongside digital strategies, to create authentic connections with audiences.

One way to plan an IRL strategy is to develop a consumer journey. For marketers, this can sometimes be a daunting, complicated process of mapping the consumer journey toward purchase. Make it simple, and grab a sheet of paper. Imagine your consumers and what a day in their life looks like. Jot down the interactions they have with media—both active and passive engagement—as well as where they go, who they talk to, etc. This will give you an idea as to how you can insert your brand message into their day, in real life.

PRO TIP

Be a deliberate observer. Go to events, engage, and take note of what's most effective, interesting, and engaging to you.

In Summary

✓ *Every sponsorship should start with an objective and purpose and end with the question "What did I get out of it?"*

✓ *Be a deliberate observer at events to see what you think works well, and then apply it to your brand.*

✓ *Align with brands with like values and similar audiences, whether it's a sponsorship or in-event collaboration.*

✓ *Ensure your brand plays an active role at events by engaging with people, not a passive display of your logo among a sea of logos.*

✓ *Ascertain that the investment of time and money is worthwhile.*

10

ALL THE
OTHER STUFF

This chapter is about the many other marketing opportunities you can use to boost your business, grow your network, and expand your reach. We included a lot of topics, so we will share just enough information for you to understand what each one is and how each one works.

However, it's important to define two things before jumping into any tactics:

- 1. Your objectives

- 2. Your strategies

Knowing what you want to achieve—specifically—and how you plan to achieve your goals will make deciding which tactics to use much easier. Going blindly into marketing can confuse the audience and waste time, effort, and money. Being prudent about where you apply your marketing efforts results in greater success. Here are the other things to consider when planning your marketing campaign.

AHA!

Trade shows and events offer excellent networking opportunities. Sometimes, the list of attendees at an event can be purchased before or after the event.

Trade Shows

Incorporating trade shows into your marketing repertoire can be an effective way to:

- Gain exposure

- Generate leads

- Build relationships

- Showcase products and services

- Launch a new product

PRO TIP

Before committing to exhibitor status at a trade show, it's often a good idea to attend a trade show as a participant to get a lay of the land and to determine whether or not it would be a valuable place to invest in having a presence.

Here's how you can leverage trade shows as part of your marketing plan:

- **Set clear objectives.** Define what success looks like.

- **Choose the right trade shows.** Research, and plan.

- **Create an engaging presence.** Design an engaging booth.

- **Offer something interactive.** Make it easy for guests to engage; offer interactive displays, contests, or live demonstrations.

- **Provide valuable content.** Address pain points and offer content, like case studies or white papers.

- **Take advantage of networking opportunities.** Be proactive in initiating conversations, and follow up after the event to nurture relationships.

> **PRO TIP**
>
> *Create your annual trade-show schedule, and develop your trade-show model that can be reused and repeated at events for consistency and efficiency. This includes the booth structure, clear and relevant messaging, visuals, the method of engagement (sampling, demo, etc.), the method for data collection, and the process for follow-up.*

Thought Leadership

Using thought leadership as a marketing tool involves positioning yourself or your brand as an authority. This approach can help you become a trusted source of expertise in your industry. Thought leadership can be a great way to:

- Gain exposure
- Showcase expertise
- Establish credibility
- Increase brand visibility
- Expand your network
- Generate trust
- Attract potential customers

Here's how you can use thought leadership as part of your marketing plan:

- **Identify your niche.** Identify your category, and define your area of expertise.
- **Create high-quality content.** Develop informative and interesting content; this can include insights and actionable advice.

- **Share insights and opinions.** Share your expertise, engage in conversations, offer solutions to common problems, or create thought-provoking perspectives.

- **Participate in speaking engagements.** Seek opportunities to speak at conferences and industry events.

- **Publish.** Conduct original research to uncover insights and trends, and publish your findings.

- **Network and collaborate.** Build relationships with other people in your industry, and uncover opportunities to do things together.

Speaking Engagements

Speaking engagements can be a great way to:

- Establish thought leadership, which is the position of being recognized as an authority or expert in a particular field or industry; speaking engagements offer a way to build your credibility as an industry expert

- Gain exposure

- Generate leads

- Build relationships

Here's how you can use speaking engagements as part of your marketing plan:

- **Identify relevant opportunities.** Pursue industry events where your audience is likely to be in attendance.

- **Craft compelling topics.** Tell stories to showcase your expertise and address current trends.

- **Create an engaging presentation.** Use an engaging and visually appealing presentation; include examples, statistics, infographics, or multimedia elements to make it more interesting.

- **Create buzz.** Use social media or email marketing to promote your speaking engagement beforehand and afterward.

- **Offer valuable content.** Give them something they can use for their own projects, like tips, strategies, and best practices.

- **Engage with the audience.** Encourage audience participation during or after the presentation.

- **Collect leads.** Follow up promptly after the event to stay top of mind and nurture relationships.

Public Relations

Public relations is the practice of managing the distribution of information between an organization or individual and the public. It involves building and maintaining a positive image or reputation through what's called "earned media channels." These channels include media relations, social media, community engagement, and events.

Public relations can be a great way to:

- Shape public perception

- Increase brand visibility

- Manage crises

- Foster positive relationships

- Enhance reputation

- Build thought leadership (this means you're recognized as an authority or expert in a particular field or industry; media opportunities for exposure offer many ways to build your credibility as an industry expert)

Here's how you can use public relations as part of your marketing plan:

- **Identify your target audience.** Identify key stakeholders, such as customers, investors, employees, media outlets, industry influencers, or community members.

- **Use storytelling.** Develop compelling narratives and story angles.

- **Share news.** Focus on stories that are newsworthy and relevant to your targeted channel of distribution.

- **Build relationships with media.** Cultivate relationships with journalists, editors, bloggers, and other media outlets that cover topics relevant to your business.

- **Leverage content marketing.** Use interesting content to educate, inform, or entertain and to showcase your expertise.

- **Participate in events.** Use events as networking opportunities to connect with people and build relationships.

- **Manage your brand's reputation.** Monitor online conversations and news coverage to identify potential issues or opportunities for proactive reputation management.

Purpose

Corporate social responsibility (CSR) can be a powerful marketing strategy for businesses to demonstrate their commitment to social and environmental issues that matter to people. Businesses usually have a defined purpose as part of their business strategy, such as supporting the local Little League or donating to a nature organization. Businesses can use their purpose-driven efforts as a marketing strategy.

CSR can be a great way to:

- Enhance brand reputation
- Attract customers

- Increase brand value

- Engage the community

- Differentiate your brand

- Build trust and loyalty

Take your approach to "giving back" beyond operations, and make it part of your marketing efforts by using these techniques:

- **Align with values.** Authenticity is key; the CSR initiatives you choose should align with your company's core beliefs so that your initiatives are genuine.

- **Communicate.** Research shows that consumers want to know what companies are doing to make things better in their world and their communities.

- **Attract customers.** Make CSR part of your brand story, emphasizing how your company is making a difference.

- **Engage employees.** Engage employees by offering volunteer opportunities or supporting causes that your employees support.

- **Selling proposition.** Use your giving strategy to create a unique selling proposition.

- **Generate publicity.** Leverage media coverage or host an event to celebrate your contributions to the community.

Networking

Networking is an invaluable skill for business and can be leveraged as a marketing strategy to:

- Generate word of mouth

- Opens doors to opportunities

- Foster meaningful connections

- Facilitate the exchange of ideas and expertise

- Expand connections

Here's how you can use networking as part of your marketing plan:

- **Establish partnerships.** Build relationships in the business community.

- **Create a list.** Determine the individuals and groups you want to connect with as part of your efforts.

- **Attend networking events.** Find events where you can meet like-minded professionals.

- **Be proactive.** When opportunities arise to make an introduction, introduce yourself.

- **Ask questions.** Be naturally curious about other people.

- **Follow up.** Send a quick note to say hello, or share a piece of information to nurture relationships.

- **Join professional organizations or volunteer.** Meet other professionals to connect with.

- **Use online networking platforms.** Ensure your profile is robust and populated; use LinkedIn to connect with and engage with other professionals (the more people who learn about you, the more reasons they have to connect with you).

- **Host networking events.** Host your own meet-up or workshop to bring together professionals in your industry.

- **Schedule one-on-one meetings.** Meet for coffee to explore potential opportunities for collaboration or business partnerships.

- **Provide value.** Share insights, resources, or other opportunities that could benefit others in your network.

- **Be real.** Be genuine, and focus on building meaningful relationships, rather than solely seeking business opportunities.

PRO TIP

Networking is not about contacting people when you need something; it's about connecting with others when you don't need anything.

PRO TIP

The personalization of a handwritten note makes a point of contact extra special.

Affiliate Marketing

Affiliate marketing is about developing partnerships through affiliates to promote your products or services in exchange for a commission. Your business can acquire reach and expand sales through the affiliate's network.

Here's what affiliate marketing can do:

- Drive sales

- Expand reach

- Increase awareness

- Enhance exposure

- Grow business

Here's how you can use affiliate marketing as part of your marketing plan:

- **Identify affiliates.** Identify potential brands that align with your brand values, target audience, and marketing objectives.

- **Recruit quality affiliates.** Look for influencers, bloggers, content creators, and other individuals or brands with a relevant audience and natural association.

- **Offer competitive commissions.** Provide attractive incentives to motivate affiliates to promote your products or services.

- **Provide marketing support.** Make it easy for affiliates to promote your products by providing easy, ready-to-use assets.

- **Communicate effectively.** Maintain frequent and useful communication by providing information about new products and promotions.

- **Offer training.** Providing training and support helps affiliates do a better job of promoting your products and services effectively.

- **Protect your reputation.** Pay attention to ensure that your affiliates adhere to your brand guidelines and values.

- **Track, and optimize.** Test different strategies to apply what's working, and stop doing whatever is not working.

Retailing and Merchandising

Retailing is the process of selling goods or services through various channels, such as physical stores, online platforms, or direct sales. It involves activities such as product selection, pricing, promotion, and distribution.

Merchandising, on the other hand, is a subset of retailing. It focuses on the selection, presentation, and promotion of products to maximize sales. Merchandising involves strategic planning and execution of product assortments, visual displays, pricing strategies, and promotional campaigns to attract customers and drive sales.

Retailing and merchandising work together to attract customers and drive sales. Here's a simple way to look at each element:

Retailing	Merchandising
Where it's sold	How it's sold
Broad idea of distribution channels	Focused idea of maximizing exposure

What retailing and merchandising can:

- Influence consumer behavior

- Enhance brand visibility

- Drive sales

- Incentivize at the point of purchase

- Motivate at the point of sale

- Create compelling in-store experiences

- Strengthen loyalty

- Contribute to the success of other marketing efforts

Here's how to leverage the retail environment as part of your marketing plan:

- **Create an appealing in-store experience.** Design space to help the consumer by highlighting featured products and guiding the customer journey.

- **Optimize product placement.** Place high-demand or high-margin products in prime locations to maximize visibility and sales.

- **Use visual appeal.** Create visually appealing spaces and eye-catching displays.

- **Use featured items.** Create areas to feature new arrivals, seasonal items, or best-selling products.

- **Use visual merchandising.** Place items in strategic places, and arrange attractive displays.

- **Use POP displays.** Leverage the check-out counter with displays to encourage impulse purchases, to add to the cart, and to increase transaction value.

- **Offer product sampling and demonstrations.** Provide opportunities for customers to interact with products firsthand.

- **Personalize the shopping experience.** Tailor the shopping experience to individual customer preferences by offering personalized recommendations.

- **Reward the best customers.** Offer loyalty programs to incentivize, and reward repeat customers.

- **Leverage signage.** Use digital signage and technology to enhance the shopping experience.

- **Cross-sell.** Implement cross-merchandising strategies with complementary products and accessories.

- **Create a sense of urgency.** Use limited-time offers, seasonal promotions, or exclusive deals to create excitement and urgency to buy.

- **Collect customer feedback.** Use feedback to make decisions and refine your approach to better meet customer needs and expectations.

....

DISTINGUISHING BETWEEN POP AND POS

Point of purchase (POP) refers to the location where a transaction occurs or where the customer buys a product or service. This could be online, in store, or through other channels.

Point of sale (POS) is specifically the physical or virtual location where the actual transaction takes place, such as a check-out counter in a retail store or an online payment gateway during an e-commerce transaction.

While they are closely related and often confused, or used interchangeably, the POP is broader and includes the entire process leading up to the sale, while the POS specifically refers to the moment when the transaction takes place.

....

Customer Service

Customer service, when done right, can create a competitive advantage for businesses. A customer-service approach to marketing can do the following:

- Build brand loyalty.
- Enhance customer satisfaction.
- Attract new business.
- Generate word-of-mouth referrals and customer advocacy.
- Attract great talent.

How to effectively use customer service to boost your business:

- **Deliver exceptional service.** Make it part of your marketing strategy, and formalize it in your brand guidelines.
- **Create positive experiences.** Anticipate customers' needs, and consistently go above and beyond to exceed their expectations.
- **Listen to your customers.** Solicit feedback, and use it to improve products, services, and processes.
- **Empower your team.** Give it the tools, training, and authority to make decisions, solve problems, and deliver exceptional service.
- **Be available.** Make it easy for customers to reach you.
- **Be accessible.** Provide options to reach you.
- **Be responsive.** Strive to provide assistance in a timely manner.
- **Educate, and inform.** Provide useful information, tips, and resources to help customers get the most out of their purchases and enhance their overall experience.
- **Resolve issues quickly.** Minimize frustration and dissatisfaction.
- **Reward loyalty.** Recognize loyal customers who advocate for your brand.

- **Promote positive reviews.** Encourage happy customers to share their positive experiences.

- **Share testimonials.** Share what someone else says about your business; this always means more to people than if you tell them yourself.

Human Resources

When you use human capital as part of your marketing strategy, it can have a meaningful impact on your business in these ways:

- Creates internal advocacy
- Creates a positive work environment
- Drives business growth
- Effects customers in a positive manner
- Builds a strong employer brand

Here's how you can use affiliate marketing as part of your marketing plan:

- **Build a strong employer brand.** This means highlighting your company culture, values, perks, and career development opportunities.

- **Invest in employee development.** Offer professional development opportunities.

- **Create a positive work environment.** Prioritize benefits and perks that prioritize employee health, happiness, and fulfillment.

- **Encourage employee advocacy.** Encourage employees to become ambassadors for your company with incentives and other perks.

- **Implement employee referral programs.** Incentivize current employees to refer qualified candidates for open positions, and encourage them to tap into their networks to help recruit top talent.

- **Highlight employee success stories.** Showcase employee accomplishments.

- **Promote diversity and inclusion.** Make these core values, and promote them as part of your employer brand.

- **Engage in CSR.** Support causes that show your commitment to making a difference beyond the bottom line.

- **Measure and improve employee satisfaction.** Continually identify areas for improvement, and make decisions to enhance the employee experience.

- **Align human resources and marketing efforts.** This creates a cohesive and compelling brand.

WARNING

Don't overlook the opportunity to leverage your employees and company culture to attract top talent, enhance brand reputation, and drive business growth. Engage employees in your marketing every step of the way so they can help support your marketing efforts.

PRO TIP

Roll in marketing efforts to employees before you roll out campaigns to consumers. Employees should know about campaigns before customers so they can rally around efforts and be part of delivering a consistent message.

Marketing Comes in Many Forms

Marketing comes in many forms tailored to different goals, target audiences, and media (methods of delivery). The world of marketing presents many options to sift through, but with clear direction and careful planning, you can assemble the right mix of marketing tools to work for you and your business.

The landscape of marketing continues to evolve with advancements in technology and changes in consumer behavior. Understanding the range of options and basic fundamental elements will enable you to better understand the changing climate and adapt accordingly. Each form of marketing offers unique opportunities to connect with the people who buy what you're selling and to make your business dreams a reality.

....

In Summary

- ✓ *Every marketing strategy and tactic should start with an objective and purpose.*
- ✓ *Try-before-you-buy product sampling instills consumer confidence.*
- ✓ *Use tracking and incorporate customer feedback to make your marketing better.*
- ✓ *Marketing comes in many forms.*

....

11

MARKETING ROUND-UP

The marketing round-up is a quick guide to what you may need to know, what you can do, and how you can apply marketing concepts to your business.

1. Gain Clarity about Your Business

- **Know:** Understand your business goals.
- **Do:** Outline your business plan. Formalize elements to hold yourself accountable.
- **Apply this to marketing:** By defining the value of your product or service and using that to drive your key messaging.

2. Know Who You Are Talking to

- **Know:** Understand who's likeliest to buy what you are selling.
- **Do:** Put definition around your primary customer.
- **Apply this to marketing:** By identifying consumer pain points and determining how your product or service can help them overcome these problems. By using the things that motivate them to buy or make a purchasing decision.

3. Use Information to Your Advantage

- **Know:** Recognize that you can use all kinds of research to drive strategies or track performance.
- **Do:** Decide what you want to know about your product or service, industry, market, or consumer to help you be more effective.
- **Apply this to marketing:** Use data and analytics to make better decisions.

4. Approach the Brand to Maximize the Value of Your Offering

- **Know:** Understand why your brand exists, what it stands for, and how it delivers for people.
- **Do:** Create a brand pyramid as a framework that serves as a snapshot of your brand's benefits, features, and attributes.
- **Apply this to marketing:** Use this information to guide your North Star in everything you do to engage with customers. Continually ask yourself, "Is this on brand?"

5. Plan for Success with Focus

- **Know:** Understand that plans are the best way to ensure actions take place in order to achieve positive outcomes.
- **Do:** A marketing plan, whether it's a single page or a comprehensive planning document.
- **Apply this to marketing:** Use the plan as an evergreen guideline. Regularly revisit and update the plan to stay on track.

6. Make Sense of Digital Marketing

- **Know:** Learn enough about digital marketing so you can navigate the options you have available to you.
- **Do:** Use specialists to help with your specific digital marketing efforts.
- **Apply this to marketing:** Start simple with a strong online presence, and build out your strategy from there, one step at a time.

7. Engage in Real Life with Promotions

- **Know:** Understand the different types of promotions available to you.
- **Do:** Find promotions that work well for what you're selling and whom you're selling to.
- **Apply this to marketing:** Start with one idea, and use a single, simple promotion over a defined period to test the response.

8. Create Content That Engages with People by Using Creative Solutions

- **Know:** Understand what you want to communicate.
- **Do:** Find a resource that can help you create assets.
- **Apply this to marketing:** Build a library of assets for efficiency and to maintain consistency in the market.

9. Reach People in the Places Where They Are

- **Know:** Sponsorships and events offer effective ways to reach consumers in places where they are already engaged.

- **Do:** Create a clear strategy for what you want to get out of sponsorships and events, and make sure your audiences are aligned between your business and their event.

- **Apply this to marketing:** Use the strategy to help guide decisions about what to be a part of, and use measurement to make sure your investment is worth it.

10. Do Some Other Stuff Too

- **Know:** Have enough understanding of the marketing tools available to you.

- **Do:** Decide which tools work best for your product or service.

- **Apply this to marketing:** Prioritize your efforts. This means not having to do many things at once. Find what works best for your business, and focus on doing it really well.

GLOSSARY

As with most industries, marketing loves to use acronyms and lingo. This is a glossary to help you better understand what these terms mean.

A/B testing: Also called "split testing" or "bucket testing"; compares two visions of content to determine which one appeals more and receives a greater response.

Activations: Execution of campaigns, events, and experiences.

Affiliate marketing: Brand partnerships in exchange for a commission or other compensation.

AI: Artificial intelligence; computer systems capable of performing complex tasks.

AI tool: A software application that uses artificial intelligence techniques.

B2B: Business to business; marketing that targets decision-makers at other businesses.

B2C: Business to consumer; marketing that targets consumers.

Brand pyramid: A simple, visual framework that outlines a brand's identity and market positioning.

Business proposal: A pitch presentation typically used to secure funding by introducing the business opportunity.

CLV (or CLTV): Customer lifetime value; a metric that indicates the total revenue a business can reasonably expect from a single customer throughout the business relationship.

Content marketing: A strategic approach focused on creating and distributing valuable, relevant, and consistent content to attract and retain customers. Instead of directly pitching products or services, it aims to provide useful information that helps customers solve their issues or meet their needs, thus building trust and establishing the brand as a thought leader in its industry.

CSR: Corporate social responsibility; a business model by which companies make an effort to operate in ways that enhance society or the environment. This organizational model can be used as a marketing strategy.

CTA: Call to action; a marketing term for what action you would like to encourage.

Customer journey: The path of interactions that a customer has with your brand, products, or services.

ESP: Emotional selling proposition; your unique emotional selling points.

Font: Style of text.

GTM: Go to market; a strategy for a business using its outside resources, to deliver its unique value proposition to customers and achieve a competitive advantage.

Influencer: An individual who has the ability to affect opinions, behaviors, or purchasing decisions of others within a specific community or audience. They typically have a significant following on social media.

IRL: In real life; outside of the digital environment.

KISS: Keep it simple, stupid; a design principle that states that designs and/or systems should be as simple as possible.

KPI: Key performance indicator; a quantifiable measure of performance over time for a specific objective.

P-value: Probability value; a statistical measure used in hypothesis testing to determine the significance of an observed result.

POP: Point of purchase; the location where a product is sold.

POS: Point of sale; the location where the payment transaction takes place.

POV: Point of view; the perspective from which the narrative is told.

Public relations: The function of managing information between an organization and the public.

Qualitative research: The anecdotal feedback received through research.

Quantitative research: Measurable information gathered by research.

Reach and frequency: The size of the audience and the number of times it is exposed to a particular piece of marketing.

ROAS: Return on ad spend; an important measurement in online mobile marketing that refers to the amount of revenue that is earned for every dollar spent on a campaign.

ROI: Return on investment; an approximate measure of an investment's profitability.

Strategy: A general plan or overall approach in achieving one or more long-term goal.

SWOT analysis: A strategic planning and management technique whose acronym stands for "strengths, weaknesses, opportunities, and threats." Strengths and weaknesses are internal factors; opportunities and threats are external factors.

Tactic: The method you use to achieve what you want.

Target audience: The demographic, psychographic, and behavioral characteristics that define the people who buy a product or service and who you market your product or service to.

Target market: This can mean the "target audience" or the geographic market in which your product or service is offered.

Thought leadership: The position of being recognized as an authority or expert in a particular field or industry.

UGC: User-generated content; published information that an unpaid contributor provides on a website, online forum, or social media platform.

USP: Unique selling proposition; the logical benefits of your product or service.

White paper: A formal document that presents a problem, issue, or topic and provides detailed analysis, research findings, and recommendations.

X: The social media platform formerly known as "Twitter."

SOURCES

A few sources used in the development of the content for this book:

Forester, Drake. "Writing Your Business Purpose (and Why It Matters)." The SCORE Association. October 12, 2023.

Forsey, Caroline. "Marketing Budget: How Much Should Your Team Spend in 2023? [By industry]." HubSpot. November 28, 2022.

Weston, Bridget. "Does Your Small Business Have a Strong Mission and Vision?" The SCORE Association. June 21, 2023.

INDEX

A

A/B testing method, 154–5
advertising and promotion
    assets, 100
    effectiveness, 40, 109
    options, 119
    social media, 101
    TV, 101
    types of, 143
affiliate marketing, 181–2, 186, 193
Airbnb pitch deck, 28
audience
    alignment, 166
    color impact, 156
    content for, 91, 153
    demographics research, 47, 50, 119,
        169
    engagement, 83, 140–2, 153, 171, 177
    identifying target, 34, 38, 45–7, 85,
        151
    influencer collaborations, 138, 140–1
    internal, employees, 48
    internal or employees, 48
    messaging for, 34, 48, 123–4, 127, 147
    preferences and behavior, 48, 52
    profile worksheet, 47
    research data on, 55
    social media content, 120, 138, 142,
        151
audio identification, 91

B

banner ads, 126
beliefs and values
    audience, 47
    cause-marketing, 138

benefits, brand pyramid, 71
brand
    added value incentives, 136
    affiliates and, 181
    affinity, 74–7
    architecture models, 87–8, 90
    assets, 94
    authority, 115
    awareness, 59, 74, 106, 109, 119, 165,
        169
    building corporate, 81
    consumer values and, 137
    CSR marketing, 179
    definition, 2
    elements of, 84–5, 94
    loyalty, 47, 74, 76–7, 185
    message of, 63, 90, 92
    message to consumer, 171
    mission and vision, 10
    organizational, 77
    on social media, 140
    value alignment, 166
    value propositions, 44
    values, 2, 37, 136, 164, 179, 181
brand guidelines, 93–5, 160, 182, 185
brand identity, 63, 92–3, 160
branded hashtags, 139
branded house, 88
branding
    conceptual, 23
    consistency in, 155, 160
    content and messaging in, 90–3
    customer journey map, 66
    goal of, 74
    guidelines for, 93–5

lifestyle, 76
loyalty vs. affinity, 74–7
vs. marketing, 73–4
personal, 77–80
sensory, 90–1, 93
brand-marketing approach, 32, 35–6,
  71–4, 155
Branson, Richard, 80–1
break-even analysis, 26
business
  brand and personal brand, 78, 95
  digital promotions, 144
  foundation for marketing, 2–4
  goals and objectives, 13, 15, 97, 102–
    3, 106–7, 110–12
  mission, 8, 12, 103
  model outlines, 2
  networking opportunities, 166
  review and update goals, 110
  support for goals, 112
  values, 10–11
business concept, 13, 24
business model, 2, 4–5, 17, 22, 30–1, 194
business plan
  concise, 24
  implementation plan, 27
  outline of, 18
  and proposal, 18
  reusing information from, 102
  template for, 24, 27
business proposal
  contents, 30–2
  format for, 32
  outline for, 29
  purpose, 3, 18
  selling concept, 27
  template for, 31
  value proposition, 91
business purpose, 3, 5–9, 197
business strategy, 16, 178
business structure, 24–5
business values, 71–2, 83, 137, 187
business venture, 17–18, 27, 80

C
cash-flow projections, 23
cash-flow statements, 26
Cathy, S. Truett, company values, 1
cause-related marketing, 136–7

Charles Schwab vision, 8
Chick-fil-A, purpose and values of, 2
color and psychology, 156–8
color palette, 93
consumer awareness, 98, 109
consumer behavior
  emotional drivers in, 40, 42
  for gain or saving, 41
  mindset, 35
  preferences, 52
  psychological factors, 39, 183
consumer demographics, 25, 103
consumer journey, for IRL strategy,
  170–1
consumers, 33. See also audience
content marketing, xii, 84, 91, 107, 116,
  118, 125, 194
cost evaluation, 165
cost structure, 17
cost-effectiveness, 20, 115
Covey, Stephen R., 43
Crayola business purpose, 6
creative assets, 94, 148–9
CSR (Corporate Social Responsibility),
  137–8, 144–5, 178, 187, 194
customer engagement, 49, 129, 135, 170
customer journey map, 66
customer service approach, 185–6

D
demographics
  in A/B testing, 154
  event marketing, 169
  PPC advertising, 121
  social media marketing, 119
  in subjective marketing, 60
  target audience, 47, 196
  targeted advertising, 115
digital marketing
  advertising for, 126–7
  components of, 117, 122
  display advertising, 126
  online presence, 117, 127, 191
  strategies, xii, 38
direct-to-consumer sales, 22
Disney business values, 1, 9, 71–3, 77

E
elevator pitch deck, 18
email marketing, xii, 120, 125, 127

emotional drivers (customers), 40
empathetic communication, 43
endorsed brand, 88
event/engagement marketing, 22, 125, 163–5, 169–70, 192
experiential marketing. *See* event marketing

F

financial statements, contents of, 23
fonts, 158–9
food, branding with, 91
funding request, business proposal, 23

G

go-to-market strategy, 21

H

Harley-Davidson's brand affinity, 75
Hershey's color use, 158
house of brand, 88
How to Write a Good Advertisement (Schwab), 40
human capital development, 186–7
human emotions, 34, 40, 42–3, 79, 153, 156, 158
human resources, 186–7
hybrid-brand model, 88

I

imagery and photography guidance, 93
implementation plan, components of, 27
incentives
    added-value, 144
    for affiliates, 181
    for consumers, 169
    in digital marketing, 116
    for employees, 186
    for feedback, 65
    on social media, 125
    use of, 186
    value-added, 136
    website sign-up, 125
interstitial ads, 126
investment. *See* funding request
investor pitch deck, 18
IRL (in real life) marketing, strategy for, 170

J

JPMorgan Chase, value focus of, 11

L

layout and design guidelines, 93
legal considerations, 94
lifestyle marketing, 37, 39, 46–7, 75
logos
    brand assets, 150
    brand identity, 76, 90, 93–4, 148, 157
    brand representation, 79, 95
    branding, 160
    design of, 158
    placement of, 166
    sponsorships and, 166, 171
    usage guidelines, 93–4
Louis Vuitton, 158
loyalty and affinity, 75

M

market dynamics, changes in, 110
market landscape, 61
marketing
    action plans for, 27
    activities for, 74, 111
    of brand, 1, 32, 35–6, 71–4, 155, 209
    budget allocation, 98
    business foundation for, 1
    campaigns and trade shows, 173
    cause-related, 136–7
    customer-service approach, 185
    design and messaging, 149
    digital, xii, 38, 107, 113–17, 122, 126–7, 191
    investment in, xiii
    personal-bias, 60
    template for plan, 110
    thought leadership for, 175
marketing goals, awareness, 166
marketing mix effects, 40
marketing plan
    affiliate marketing use in, 181, 186
    creating, 102
    networking for, 180
    public relations in, 178
    retail environment for, 183
    review of goals, 110
    scope of, 190
    speaking engagements in, 176
    thought leadership in, 175
    trade show use in, 174

marketing process
  activities for, xi–xiii
  defined, xi
  emotions in, 34, 42–3, 156
  engaging audience, 83, 106, 140–2,
      153, 171, 177
  goals, xii–xiii
  ongoing, 51
marketing strategies
  activities for, xii–xiv
  cost-effective, 40, 97–101
  developing, 51–3, 60–1
  external factors and, 37
  human resources in, 186
marketing tools, 175, 188, 192
merchandising, 183–4
merchandising and retailing, 182–3
messaging
  creative, 152–3
  effective, 123–4
  guidelines, 94
  targeted, 113, 115, 169

N
native ads, 126
networking, in-person, 126

O
online and digital marketing
    strategies, xii
operations plan, 23

P
pay-per-click (PPC) advertising, 117, 121
personal bias, avoiding, 60, 68
personal brands, 77–81, 87, 95
personal-bias marketing, 60
personality, 37, 39, 46–7, 80, 93, 142, 158
perspectives
  of consumer, 5, 43
  thought-provoking, 176
pitch deck, 18, 27–31, 91, 94
platforms
  digital sales, 113, 115, 121
  online networking, 180
  primary brand, 87
  real-time bidding, 127
  showcase brand products, 163
  for social goals, 119
  video streaming, 114

POP (point of purchase), 184, 195
POV (consumer point of view), 3
PPC (pay-per-click) advertising, 117, 121
pricing strategy, xii, 22, 25, 106
programmatic ads, 127
promotions
  basic types and benefits, 130, 143
  customer engagement, 129
  designing, 145
  social media, 138–9, 142, 144
psychographic, target audience, 47
purchase decision influences, 39–44

R
referral programs, 125
remarketing ads, 127
reputation of brand, 50, 136, 178
research
  on competitors, 104
  for consumer preferences, 136
  conclusions from, 67
  conducting, 62
  custom, 54
  for customer preferences, 179
  data and analytics and, 53
  to drive strategies, 190
  existing, 54
  first-party, 58
  foundational for marketing, 59–60
  insights from data, 55, 60
  as investment, 53
  key areas of, 51
  methodologies, 54, 58, 109
  objectivity in, 60
  primary and secondary, 55
  process of investigation, 58
  in product life cycle, 51
  qualitative vs. quantitative, 195
  scrappier side of, 59
  selecting questions for, 58
  for strategies and performance, 190
  for understanding customers, 68
resources
  allocation, 107, 111
  creative, 149
  free, 125
  limited, xiv
  unlimited, xiv
retailing and merchandising, 182–3

revenue
    forecast, 23, 98, 168
    streams, 17
    total, 194
reward programs, 49, 58, 125, 131, 133,
        140, 143, 184
rich-media ads, 126
risk analysis, 23, 27
risk-reward equation factor, 60

S
sales approach, 22
sales promotions, 49, 142
Schwab, Victor O., 40
scrappy, xiv, 20, 51
search engine optimization (SEO), xii
seasonal promotions, 133, 143, 184
selling, in marketing process, xi
sensory-branded experience, 91
services to customers. *See* customer
        services
signage
    digital, 184
    effective, 159–60
    promotional, 148
    sponsorship and, 165
social media
    content sharing, 119
    marketing, xii, 40, 126
    platforms, 107, 119–20, 126, 138, 144,
        196
    polls, 140
    posts, 119, 148
    promotions, 138–9, 142, 144
sound logos, 91
speaking engagements, 176
sponsorships
    benefits of, 164–9
    cost-effectiveness of, 163
    logo placement, 166
    opportunities, 163–4
subjective marketing, 60

T
thought leadership, as marketing tool,
        175
Tiffany Blue Boxes, 73
top-of-mind relevance, 91
trade shows, 174
typography guidelines, 93

U
usage examples, 94
user-generated content (UGC), 139, 196

V
valuation vs. evaluation, 165
value exchange, 3
value proposition, 22, 44, 106, 124
values
    for business model, 2
    of Chick-fil-A company, 1
    from consumer point of view, 3
    defining, 32
    delivered, 84
    member feedback, 66
    in organization's behavior, 3
    perceived, 22
video ads, 126
visibility, signage, 159
visual appeal, 183
visual communications, 93
visual identity, 90, 93, 147
visual representation, 116
voice and tone recommendations, 94

W
webinars, 125
website sign-up forms, 125
Whole Foods business values, 11, 157
Winfrey, Oprah, 81
worksheet
    budget-builder, 101
    business plan template, 24
    business proposal template, 31
    business purpose, 6
    competitive analysis, 104
    creating email subject, 123
    customer-survey starter, 65
    marketing-plan template, 110
    mission, vision, and values, 12
    personal-brand, 84
    promotion evaluation, 134–5
    sponsorship evaluation, 164
    target audience profile, 47

ABOUT THE AUTHORS

SCOTT HARKEY is CEO of THE HARKEY GROUP, a collection of agencies meeting the needs of the modern marketer.

One of the Harkey Group agencies, O.H. Partners—the largest independent full-service agency in the Southwest U.S.—has landed on *Inc.* magazine's list of the fastest-growing private companies since 2018, has been named one of the 100 fastest-growing advertising agencies in the country, and has been recognized as the number-one advertising agency in Arizona.

Scott's genuine passion to grow and elevate is reflected in his visionary approach, forward-thinking work, and successful leadership. Scott is a speaker and the host of the *Rebrand Podcast.*

AMY COLBOURN is Managing Director of MONOGRAM, one of the HARKEY GROUP agencies and a boutique specialty brand agency in Las Vegas serving the hospitality and casino industry specifically.

Amy's passion is branding and brand marketing. Her true superpower lies in identifying the competitive advantage in even the most saturated markets and defining a reason to believe at the most conceptual stages of a place's existence. In 2024, Amy's first book, *Awareness Is Overrated: And Other Provocative Ideas About Marketing,* was published.

THE HARKEY GROUP™

▬ READY TO CREATE VALUE ON DAY ONE

THE HARKEY GROUP was built to meet the evolving needs of ambitious marketers intent on growth, determined to improve their brand's customer experience, and insistent on crushing yesterday's benchmarks. It's a full-service, integrated marketing organization with multiple consumer-centric, performance-focused, and creatively-inspired agencies, each prepared to tackle even the most complex marketing challenges. By partnering with some of the world's most esteemed brands across a variety of industry verticals, we've received countless industry awards in branding, advertising, public relations, social media, and production.

OTHER TITLES IN THE KM PRESS FAMILY OF BOOKS

KEN MCELROY

ABCs of Real Estate Investing
The Secrets of Finding Hidden Profits Most Investors Miss

ABCs of Buying Rental Property
How You Can Achieve Financial Freedom in Five Years

ABCs of Property Management
What You Need to Know to Maximize Your Money Now

Advanced Guide to Real Estate Investing
How to Identify the Hottest Markets and Secure the Best Deals

The Sleeping Giant
The Awakening of the Self-Employed Entrepreneur

Return to Orchard Canyon
A Business Novel

BLAIR SINGER

Sales Dogs
You Don't Have to Be an Attack Dog to Explode Your Income

Team Code of Honor
The Secrets of Champions in Business and in Life

Summit Leadership
Taking Your Team to the Top

Little Voice Mastery
How to Win the War Between Your Ears in 30 Seconds or Less and Have an Extraordinary Life

JOHN MACGREGOR

The Top Ten Reasons the Rich Go Broke
Powerful Stories That Will Transform Your Financial Life . . . Forever

RICH FETTKE

The Wise Investor
A Modern Parable About Creating Financial Freedom and Living Your Best Life

MIKE MALONEY

Guide to Investing in Gold & Silver
Protect Your Financial Future

CHAD KERBY AND TK STRATTON

Speak and Get What You Want
Communicate Like the World's Most Successful Leaders

STRATEGIES SERIES

Legal Strategies for Everyone
The Complete Guide to Covering Your Assets, Maximizing Wealth, and Protecting Your Family

Tax Strategies for Everyone
How to Slash Your Taxes and Build Wealth

Sales Strategies for Everyone
Essential Selling Tips From the Sales Coach You Wish You Had

Marketing Strategies for Everyone
Everything You Need to Know Without Having to Know Everything

NEW AND COMING SOON FROM KM PRESS

Real Estate Strategies for Everyone
Ten Great Ways to Get Started in Real Estate Investing

KM PRESS